The Tang
Campaign

To all ranks of the regular army, past and present, and particularly those whose regiments, whatever their present names, bear on their colours the first honour of all, Tangier

The Tangier Campaign

A.J. SMITHERS

TEMPUS

First published 2003

Tempus Publishing Limited
The Mill, Brimscombe Port,
Stroud, Gloucestershire, GL5 2QG

© National Army Museum, 2003

The right of National Army Museum to be identified as
the Author of this work has been asserted in accordance
with the Copyrights, Designs and Patents Act 1988.

All rights reserved. No part of this book may be reprinted
or reproduced or utilised in any form or by any electronic,
mechanical or other means, now known or hereafter invented,
including photocopying and recording, or in any information
storage or retrieval system, without the permission in writing
from the Publishers.

British Library Cataloguing in Publication Data.
A catalogue record for this book is available from the British Library.

ISBN 0 7524 2582 X

Typesetting and origination by Tempus Publishing Limited
Printed in Great Britain by Midway Colour Print, Wiltshire

Contents

That extraordinary siege, where a handful of English red-coats, unpaid and ill-fed, fought a breached and broken town against countless hordes for the honour of their King during twenty years.

'Mr Mitchelbourne's Last Escapade', 1900
A.E.W. Mason

Preface

Two elements conspire to make writing history of any part of the seventeenth century more difficult than it need be. Consider the first. Somewhere or other the Duke of Marlborough is on record as saying that he was thankful that he spelt like a gentleman and not like a damned pedant. Piercy Kirke's letter to Lord Dartmouth of 29 April 1681 begins:

> I thinck need not give you the truble of recommending Maior Pope for I am shuer you are so well satesfide he is yr humble servant, that you will doe him and the Regement all the faivour you can and if you will doe me the honour to let His Royall Highnesse know I am only heare to sarfe him and as he his maid me I will for ever continue his true and faithfull servant

and so on with abbreviations to match. The Tangier State Papers are in much the same style. To follow them slavishly would, in my view, make reading a laborious business; it seems hard, after hours of ploughing through matter of this kind, to realise that the writers spoke English much as you and I do.

The other factor is dates. The calendar year changed its number on 25 March. Thus something that happened on 20 March 1670, as we would reckon it, will be dated in original papers as 20 March 1669. Continental dates were ten days ahead of our own until 1752.

To produce a narrative that I hope to be readable I have converted all dates into those in current use. By the same token I have frequently altered spellings to come into line with modern practice. In doing so, however, I have not had the hardihood to alter a word of the original text. Our ancestors, better educated in the Classics than most of us, do not deserve such impertinence.

When it comes to expressing opinions of men long dead it may be wise to remember Sir Charles Oman's view. Writing in old age he observed that:

> It is now quite usual for me to detect those of the younger generation writing down as 'history' those lucubrations on matters that to me are not history but 'things seen', and judging at second hand men who to me are well-remembered definite individuals whom one had studied and sometimes interviewed. Often the verdicts of the present generation seem to me unconvincing.

One can only make what one can from the raw material available.

Acknowledgements

To my friend Martin Marix-Evans whose help with and touching faith in the merits of this book propelled it into existence, to two gentlemen of Whitby, Mr John Gaskin and Mr Charles Forgan who were kind enough to add much to my knowledge of the work and their predecessors there in building the Great Mole and to Mr Adrian Webb of the United Kingdom Hydrographic Office for information of a seafaring nature connected with the same masterpiece of engineering.

Introduction

Though the aphorism is widely disdained it remains a fact that history does repeat itself, sometimes. And it is certainly true that as wars produce armies so, quite often, do unemployed or underemployed armies produce wars. The evidence for this, in our own country, is strong. The Norman Conquest ensured that, for a long time to come, English soldiers with no patriotic interest at stake fought on the European mainland for the purpose of seating such French intruders as then occupied the English throne upon that of France also. Eventually there came the Hundred Years' War, ending in 1453 with the expulsion of the English and their grudging return to their own island. The consequence of this, though foreseeable, was disagreeable to their countrymen. England was soon overrun with knights and archers, trained and accustomed to war, out of work and ripe for mischief. Nor was it a matter only of lawless individuals. The companies that had for so long preyed upon the French were often kept together by their masters, confident in the knowledge that there would be plenty for them to do. There was, and Macaulay tells of it.

> Cooped up once more within the limits of the island, the
> warlike people employed in civil strife those arms which had
> been the terror of Europe and the great lords, unable to

gratify their tastes by plundering the French, were eager to plunder each other.

It must have almost been a relief to the common folk when, after a couple of years, the Wars of the Roses began in the streets of St Albans and brigandage took on a more or less recognisable shape.

The wars, hard fought for undeserving leaders, proved once again a truism. Only trained regular troops, equipped with the best weapons going, could expect to become masters of a battlefield. Barnet, Tewkesbury and the other very bloody fields were fought out in the main by professionals loyal to their paymasters. No ordinary shire levies could have stood for long before the arrow storm. The regular soldier was king.

With the coming of the Tudors the need for the regular soldier seemed to have passed. For a long time to come it was the navy, Royal and Merchant alike, upon whom the health and safety of the realm depended. The land forces had only one bright spot during the long conflict with an imperial Spain. On 1 May 1572 the Queen, at Greenwich, reviewed a body of some 300 gentlemen who, under Captain Thomas Morgan, had volunteered to take service under the Dutch. Many years were to pass and many feats of arms were to be carried out by them and their successors before they would return to the royal service under the proud name of the Buffs. It was a merciful providence that absolved the willing but not very effective English shire levies from having to take on the dreaded Spanish *tercios*[1] aboard the Armada.

The world continued to move on and once again it recognised an English regular army. History remembers it under the name of the New Model Army and ties it to the fratricidal wars of Charles and Cromwell. Its story, however, does not end there. Cromwell's red-coats, as well as invading islands in the West Indies, returned to Europe and revived memories of Crécy, Poitiers and Agincourt. They also introduced into the mouths of their countrymen names that would burn into the minds of generations far distant. On 24 May 1658, under command of Turenne and for once allied with the French, 6,000 red-coats trounced the Spaniard on the dunes of Dunkirk, marching on from there to lay siege first to Bruges and then to Ypres. There, under another Captain Morgan, they stormed the city in such style that Turenne himself embraced Morgan and called him 'one of the bravest captains of the time'. The Menin Gate panels cannot list all the English dead thereabout who have no known grave. Having watched the Spanish garrison march out of Ypres, the English, their work done, were withdrawn to Dunkirk. The town was retained partly for sentimental reasons but its new garrison had little joy from it. They endured a winter of cold, want and misery, much of it brought on by every man's deep anxiety about what the future would hold for good soldiers.

The Restoration promised well. By a supreme financial effort the New Model Army, by then down to about 50,000 men, was paid off and demobilised. For probably the first time in history such disbandment went off perfectly smoothly. On 24 May 1660 Sir Edward Hyde told Parliament that:

> No other Prince in Europe would be willing to disband such an army, an army to which victory is entailed, and which, humanly speaking, could hardly fail of conquest, an army whose order and discipline, whose sobriety and manners, whose courage and success, hath made it famous and terrible over the world.

Macaulay tells of what happened instead of the orgies of crime that had followed such affairs in the past.

> In a few months there remained not a trace indicating that the most formidable army in the world had just been absorbed into the mass of the community none was charged with any theft or robbery, none was heard to ask for alms, and that if a baker, a mason, or a waggoner attracted notice by his diligence and sobriety, he was in all probability one of Oliver's old soldiers.

The King, being under the necessity of having at least a small army, set about seeing what could be done. It was during the next few years that, by one means or another, the army that the British – no longer just the English – people of the present time know came into its earliest form of existence. The temper of the King's subjects was not universally friendly. All the praises heaped by modern historians on the New Model Army are merited but not all of its contemporaries would have wanted to see it back again. The rule of the major-generals was too recent not to arouse loathing for military men. Nevertheless, the King, lacking any sort of a police force, needed as a matter of security to be protected in his person, crown and dignity – as the words of the soldier's oath put it – against all enemies. The slightly dotty Fifth Monarchy men provided the counter-weight. When they raised their insurrection in January 1661 they began in London. No civil power being able to put it down it was left to Monck's regiment of the New Model Army, on its way to disbandment, to see them off. The King seized the opportunity. Monck's regiment marched to Tower Hill, laid down its arms and immediately took them up again as a regiment of the Foot Guards. Thus the Coldstream came into being. The King's other Household Regiment, under Colonel Russell, already existed and had taken into its ranks those Cavaliers who had fought against the red-coats at Dunkirk Dunes but refused to surrender to foreigners. They, as the sovereign's personal body, became the First Guards. The name Grenadiers would come later. To round the brigade off came two regiments of horse, the ex-Cavaliers who became the Life Guards and the former Cromwellian cavalry which was to become known as the Blues. It was a useful start. The Infantry of the Line began with the arrival in 1662, courtesy of Louis XIV, of his Scotch Brigade, intended as a further defence against Fifth Monarchy men and their like. It came into the army list in that year as the Royal Scots but returned to France soon afterwards and only came permanently into the records in 1670.

It was very much a home-service army, although beginning to bear a strong resemblance to the one known to the last few generations of Englishmen. Because of its proximity to the throne its members, even in the lowest ranks, were men of some standing. The Life Guards, who stood and still stand at the head of the Army List, took precedence of everybody and were known for at least the next century as 'gentlemen of the Life Guards'; the next in seniority began its new existence as Lord Oxford's Regiment; when the title became the Blues – the Royal Horse Guards – it could still claim an ancestry going back to the honoured named of Vere. The first troopers of the Blues were drawn from the pick of the New Model Army; red and blue were to settle down together as blue and grey were to do after another and greater civil war. At the other end of the military scale the county militias were re-organized under the lords lieutenant with the returned King being acknowledged as supreme commander of all forces of land and sea.

Though the professional forces now looked like, and were, a regular army they were plainly top-heavy, being Household troops and little else. The expansion of the infantry of the line, and the exhausting business of finding recruits for overseas, was about to begin. On 21 May 1662 King Charles, with the blessing of his brother monarch Louis XIV, took as his wife the Portuguese Princess Catherine of Braganza. With her came a considerable and welcome dowry. The promise of half a million pounds sterling was a good start, free trade with Brazil and the Portuguese East Indies suggested riches to come and there were pieces of real estate that would have to be examined. The island of Bombay was too far distant for London to have a lot to do with its affairs; the East India Company, dating from 1599, had been given a new charter in 1661 enabling it, amongst other things, to raise an army of its own[2]. That ought to take care of Bombay. Tangier would be another matter. The Portuguese Ambassador, in the course of negotiating for the marriage, had offered to 'assign over to the Crown of England forever the possession of Tangier, a place likely to be of great benefit and security to the trade of England'. Portugal had been the first of the European powers to explore the

remoter parts of the world and to, in some fashion, fortify and settle in many far away places with strange sounding names; Portugal
was now plainly in decline and, like subsequent empires, was finding herself with quite a lot of unwanted property rich with moral
obligations but otherwise lacking charm. All the same, with
England's now considerable interests in the New World where her
future seemed to lie, a port on the Atlantic coast might well be
something worth having.

It would, of course, need a garrison, even though money was
tight, but in 1661, the effort seemed well worth making.

I

The Dowry

The idea of having a possession in this part of Africa was greeted by enthusiasm all round. It was an age of empire building amongst the British, and the earlier empire, upon which the sun never set, that of Spain, was manifestly in decline. Not enough, however, to keep it a good neighbour to the descendants of Henry the Navigator. The long wars with France, in open field and in traditional Spanish guerrilla fashion, had ended in 1661 with the Treaty of the Pyrenees and the opportunity seemed to have come for another stab at Portugal. It could well have been a home thrust, but King Charles the bridegroom was more than a mere walking gentleman in the long play of Europe. A small army was scraped together – few details remain of how it was made up but New Model veterans were available – and sent post-haste to Lisbon. For the first, but not the last, time since John of Gaunt and his archers had saved Portugal in 1383 a British army made itself felt in the Peninsula. In the battle at Ameixai in the Alemtejo the invading Spaniards were routed. The gratitude of the House of Braganza was welcome but the campaign had swallowed up nearly all of Queen Catherine's half-million. Not that it had all been paid in cash to begin with.

When the time arrived for the Princess to be escorted to her new home the King had chosen for his emissary one of the best men of his day. Edward Montagu was a man of fine presence and distinguished record, even though he had not always been a King's man. At the age of nineteen he had commanded a regiment of the

New Model Army at Naseby with outstanding courage, a quality which he had shown again in September 1645 at the storming of Bristol. Though he had become a close friend to Cromwell he had quitted the army after the First Civil War and had avoided any part in the proceedings that led up to the execution of Charles I, an action of which he was known to have strongly disapproved. Under the Commonwealth he had taken to the sea and served under Blake in the Mediterranean where he won a good reputation as a self-taught admiral. His part in bringing the King into his own again was well known and probably dictated by the sensible consideration that monarchy was better than anarchy rather than by enthusiasm for the House of Stuart. His private life, unlike most, was irreproachable and he could be trusted to deal both honourably and intelligently with whatever problems might confront him. On arrival at Lisbon Montagu, recently created Earl of Sandwich, found matters to be not quite as they had been represented at Whitehall. He wrote to Lord Clarendon about having spent 200,000 crowns on the fleet – the Portuguese crown was worth about five shillings – and that 'there is 400,000 in sugar, plate and jewels on board and 800,000 more in Bills of Exchange to be paid two months after wedlock'. The King had not bargained for the dowry being paid in grocery and table decorations but the bride's mother was a cautious woman. Queen Regent Luisa was Spanish born, the daughter of the Duke of Medina Sidonia of Armada fame, and she was in no position to be over-generous with the scanty assets of the kingdom to which she had succeeded on the death of her husband John of Braganza. Being a devout Catholic she probably shared the views of her subjects about the deviant religion of her future son-in-law but she knew enough of King Charles by reputation to be sure that it was not in his nature to haggle with a lady, especially over money matters. It does not appear that the missing part of the dowry was ever paid but with so many set-offs it is impossible to be dogmatic about it.

The orders given to Lord Sandwich included one to pay a visit to Algiers before returning home in order to patch up some sort of peace with the pirate-king who ruled that place. On 31 July 1661 his squadron arrived off the port only to be told by the English Consul that Mr Parker, a merchant of Mark Lane, had recently been captured by corsairs and was held there. Lord Sandwich tried to be conciliatory but the Algerians answered that he would have no peace unless they were permitted to continue searching English ships. Blake's old lieutenant was having none of this and warped his ships into position. A few broadsides were put into the town but the east wind called the Levanter brought on so rough a sea that few hits were scored. It was, however, a show of force sufficient to secure the release of Mr Parker[3]. The warning having been given, Lord Sandwich weighed anchor and returned to Lisbon to collect up the rest of the fleet and to bring Princess Catherine to a belated landing after a long, rough journey at Portsmouth. Before long he was in trouble with both bride and groom, each accusing him of misrepresentation of the character and person of the other. He appears to have taken this very hard and was for a time seriously ill, though Pepys asserts that it was nothing worse than influenza.

On 21 May 1661 the marriage was duly celebrated and the King assumed the lawful (in European eyes) title to, amongst other places, 'Our City of Tangier'[4].

On first acquaintance the place did not seem to have much to offer. There were no known deposits of silver or gold. The irrigation works built by the Romans had long fallen into disuse. Three distinct ridges of the Atlas Mountains crossed the Moroccan hinterland, the plains between them being of high fertility. The American newspaperman Stephen Bonsal spent his honeymoon there a little over a couple of centuries later and wrote with amazement of what he saw.

> Where agriculture is practised it is with the most primitive implements and in the crudest fashion imaginable. Yet such is the richness of the soil, the crops are often enormous. It is only the fanaticism and the folly of its present rulers that prevents Morocco from becoming once again as it was for five or six centuries the granary of Europe[5].

It could have been written at practically any time during the preceding thousand years.

The potential of Tangier lay in two things: as a regular port, once the harbour facilities had been improved, it would make the Royal Navy master of the Western Mediterranean. If fate were kind it might also be the nucleus of a Christian kingdom amongst the warring and barbarous tribes of what had once been Mauretania Tingitensis. The commission given to its first governor, Lord Peterborough, was optimistic in its instructions.

> Whereas we intend forthwith to settle and secure our City of Tangier and the Territories and Dominions adjacent in or near the Coasts of Barbary or the Kingdoms of Sus, Fez and Morocco, some or one of them in the continent of Africa. And for that purpose have resolved by and with the advice of our Privy Council forthwith to raise, draw forth and transport thither such forces of horse and foot as we shall judge necessary for our service in the defence of the said City of Tangiers and our dominions and territories in or near to the said Kingdoms of Sus, Fez and Morocco.

Lord Peterborough was plainly not intending to immure himself. Having been appointed captain-general of all the forces in the city there was laid on him the additional duty of employing any local forces he could muster and:

> if need should require... to lead them forth against any enemies, rebels or traitors and them to fight, kill and slay and subdue to our obedience and to invade, surprise and reduce such towns, forts, castles or countries as shall declare or maintain any hostility against us or that may endanger the peace or security of our City or territories aforesaid and to possess and strengthen them with forts or garrisons, raze, dismantle or disable them.

The tenor of the instructions was clear. Any local leader who might manifest hostility to the new regime must run the risk of having his country taken from him and added to the new dominion by force of arms. Provided, of course, that sufficient force was available to Lord Peterborough or his successors.

The choice of Henry Mordaunt, second Earl of Peterborough, as captain-general of Tangier suggests that the King was at pains to heal old wounds and to deal fairly between unrepentant Cavaliers and reformed Parliament men. His father had been given his title by Charles I but, at the outbreak of the Civil War, he had accepted a commission as general of the Ordnance under the Earl of Essex. Fate, however, got in first and Peterborough died on 18 June 1642 before he had had the opportunity to perform any action worth mentioning. His son at the age of eighteen found himself immured in the ranks of the Parliamentary army in the days before the New Model Army but rapidly came to the conclusion that this was no place for him. In April 1643 he deserted to the King at Oxford and in September of the same year he was badly wounded at Newbury in command of a regiment. For a long time he was *hors de combat* but in 1647, after a brief meeting with his captive King, he joined with the Duke of Buckingham and the Earl of Holland to raise the Royal Standard again at Dorking. Their little force was easily dispersed by Cromwell, and Peterborough, severely wounded for the second time, was fortunate to be able to escape to Antwerp. From there he conducted negotiations which led to his compounding his former estate and in 1649, after the death of the King, he returned home. Between that time and the Restoration in 1660 Henry Mordaunt disappeared from history but it is hard to believe that a young man of such spirit and devotion to his sovereign was idle.

It is not certain when he first met Edward Montagu, who was of almost exactly the same age, but once the Interregnum was over and the King on his throne again they became firm friends. Montagu – or Sandwich as he must henceforth be called – knew Spain, Portugal and the Barbary Coast and had a rare combination of experience as soldier and sailor.

It should then come as no surprise to learn that the Articles of War drawn up by the Cavaliers followed word for word those of the New Model Army. The list of very practical questions as to the extent of Peterborough's authority which were submitted to the King for his instructions may very well have owed much to the suggestions of Lord Sandwich. Very possibly he also helped to prepare the answers which were clear as they could be in the face of so many imponderables.

On the domestic side the captain-general was granted plenary powers. He was made vice admiral, with express power of command over all naval forces that might from time to time be about the city; he was to set up a Prize Court, to nominate his own judges, to establish Courts Martial with power of life and death over all inhabitants, to make laws 'as near as may be conformable to the laws of England, to levy taxes out of which the garrison was to be maintained and to give an account of them once a year.' In addition there were nine points of precise instruction. Lord Peterborough was to have the two regiments, one of foot and one of horse, which were to be raised specifically for African service as well as two from Dunkirk which would be returned to their natural allegiance in exchange for five million livres. He was to receive the city and country with its artillery from the Portuguese governor and to 'endeavour to take into the King's service such Portugal horse as are willing to continue there', to set up a free port and to build a mole. On no account was the pay of the soldiers to be used to support the inhabitants. No new governor of a freshly acquired province could have asked for more.

Unfortunately the state of Tangier was far removed from the description of it given to the council in Whitehall. Once, long ago, it had been an important part of the empire of Carthage, master of the western Mediterranean for more than six centuries; Scipio Africanus had left it in ruins after the Third Punic War in AD 146 and for nearly 300 years after that it had thriven as a Roman colony, in the interior the deserted ruins of the Roman town of Volubilis serving as a permanent reminder of the country's potential under a settled government.

From Rome it had passed in the fifth century to the Vandals, it had been briefly returned to New Rome by Belisarius in AD 533 and in AD 698 the swift camel-borne armies of Islam had moved in never to be expelled. From the hills the Rock of Tariq which we call Gibraltar is plain to see, a view of the bridge over which the armies of the Prophet surged into Europe in AD 711, unstoppable until they met the Frankish swordsmen of Charles Martel outside Poitiers more than twenty years later. It was a European enclave in an Arab world since it had been stormed by Alfonso of Portugal in 1471, a mere fourteen years after the Byzantine Empire had finally gone down under the guns of the conquering Turks. The great days of the Arab Emirates of Seville and Cordoba had long since ceased to be more than a memory; a memory of days when Arabic was the tongue of men most learned in the sciences and which remained present only in such words as algebra, alcohol and the names of the planets[6].

Since 1492, the year which saw the end of Islam in Europe with the conquest of Granada and the first glimpse of a great world to the west, the North African littoral had lapsed into a series of pirate strongholds, factions warring constantly against each other and under pressure from the slow, relentless, westward movement of the Ottoman Turks. Their repulse from Malta by the Knights under Grand Master La Vallette in 1565 had been followed by the great galley battle off Lepanto seven years later, in the course of which Don John of Austria had smashed the Turkish fleet and deprived it of its power to do mischief for some time to come. The southern Mediterranean was still an Arab lake dominated by small fore and aft rigged pirate craft that could out-manoeuvre and board the round ships of European merchants with uncomfortable ease. A series of unhappy experiences, however, had demonstrated to them that European warships might be clumsy but their guns could smash any galley or xebec that might come within range. The fighting ships were left untroubled, but the merchantmen were in permanent danger of losing their cargoes and contributing yet more slaves to the oars of their persecutors. Many decades were to pass before this plague was ended.

By the time of the marriage negotiations of King Charles and Princess Catherine the Portuguese hold on Tangier had weakened. No more than a town of some 500 houses, one great church, a convent, nine chapels and a dilapidated castle overlooking more dilapidated walls remained; within them lived between 4,000 and 5,000 people, well over sixty per cent of them women and children. Not for the last time were the attractions of Tangier a little over-stated for the benefit of strangers. Lord Peterborough's first despatch from 'The Castel of Tangier', written on 17 February 1661, a few days after he landed, told of the place being:

> so full of spoil, scarcity and want as to all such utensils as could have given assistance to English soldiers... had not His Lordship (Sandwich) continued his care after we were possessed as well as he did before for fuel, timber, instruments for our artillery and several other things of which the place as well as we were destitute I know not to what extremes we should have come. The Portuguese... will soon all be gone and carry away with them all other materials of economy and household subsistence to the very floors, the windows and the doors.

The fact of the matter was that Tangier had continued to be held by the Portuguese only because it was a useful trading post for the Moors and none of their rulers for a long time past had felt inclined to mount a serious assault against it. None of this was apparent when King Charles signed Peterborough's commission on 6 September 1661.

Quite a lot was known about Tangier, for every substantial power in Europe had had for many years its trading establishments, complete with full consular apparatus, at every place of importance throughout the Mediterranean. The most significant piece of information by far was that the very existence of the place was precarious and that the hostile tribesmen round about might at any time combine and try to take it by storm. Its defence was not something to be entrusted to raw levies, but there was little money left and searches had to be made amongst the reserves of trained but temporarily ineffective troops available.

The first place to look was, of course, in Dunkirk. The glorious Six Thousand were much depleted in numbers and the nationalities that had fought it out on the dunes were now less distinguishable from each other than they had been a couple of years before. The town of Dunkirk had been vacated by the Spaniards soon after the fall of Ypres. The unemployed soldiers had at any rate somewhere to live, says Fortescue, 'there were certain buildings called the barracks or Spanish quarters'. It was the first time the word appeared in print and it would be long before one might read of barracks again. But there they lived, including in the beginning the 300 or so Cavaliers that made up the English King's Royal Regiment of Guards, under Condé, who had very reluctantly surrendered to their countrymen on the sandhills. By 1662 they had long since returned home, to become a part of their King's household troops. Those remaining seem to have included what was left of Dillon's Irish Regiment, men who had fled from the wrath of Cromwell, along with others from the three Irish regiments – the Duke of York's, Lord Bristol's and Lord Ormonde's – who had fought against them but were now comrades in adversity. The muster rolls were so falsified that no certainty is possible about numbers, but the Dunkirk garrison, which volunteered almost to a man to serve at Tangier rather than be turned out to starve, was a valuable nucleus of tried and veteran troops. Lord Peterborough must have welcomed them. Dunkirk itself, that notorious pirates' nest, continued in English hands for a little longer, its sale to France being one of the nails in the coffin of Sir Edward Hyde, by then Lord Clarendon[7].

The greater part of the garrison, well practised in the defence of beleaguered fortresses, would find no novelty in guarding the walls of another in a superior climate. Or so it was reasonable to expect. Long service in foreign climates was something that would become familiar to British soldiers as time went by; Tangier sounded, at the least, much better than Jamaica.

Mr Secretary Nicholas, who had been born in the reign of Elizabeth I and was shortly to retire, was kept busily employed in drawing up establishments, complete with details of rates of pay.

The final one, signed and dated 9 October 1661, set out exactly what would be allowed to 'the Lord General': two regiments of foot each 1,000 strong, two more at half that number and a troop of 100 horse only. The artillery was to be six gunners, six gunners' mates and twelve 'matrosses' to take over the weapons bequeathed by the Portuguese. The total cost would be £70,609 13s 4d, plus another, £778 9s 2d for the troop of eighty Portugal horse and their officers. This very large sum, about as much as the King received from all sources during the first year of his interrupted reign, was really no more than an arithmetical exercise suited to the tidy civil service mind. Nobody knew whether the taxes and other revenues of Tangier would be worth anything and, in any event, there would be no question of much of the money ever being paid. The garrison would think itself fortunate if enough money dribbled regularly through to keep it from actual want. Even so, to a demobilised and jobless veteran, service with the Colours meant at least comradeship and fairly regular meals. At this point of time it is impossible to find out what proportion of the recruits to the new regular army were old Parliamentary men but, judging by the alacrity with which they settled down under very strange conditions, it is fair to suppose that they made up a majority. No Christian could object to joining an army whose avowed purpose was to fight the heathen Moor even though the only two chaplains on the strength were Church of England men. The ranks were filled almost at once. Colonels Kingwell, Harley and Farrell were well satisfied. 'None did ever go to sea upon any foreign design with greater willingness and courage than that Regiment of English (from Dunkirk) so that in this one regiment there are 1244 veteran soldiers beside officers' was the view expressed in *Mercurius Publicus* when they embarked on their journey on 9 December.

The voyage was uneventful. Probably, as they sailed past the Goodwin Sands some of the older hands would have remarked the spot where General Reynolds, the original commander of the Six Thousand, had been driven ashore and drowned leaving Sir Robert Lockhart to fight the battle of The Dunes. One may also imagine the feelings of officers who had never seen a Moor in their lives being under the necessity of lecturing their men about what might lie in store for them, in much the same way as their remote descendants who had never seen a Japanese person were to perform the same office for soldiers on their way to join General Slim's Fourteenth Army.

No illustration seems to have come down of the uniforms issued to the rank and file but one of an officer of the Tangier foot in 1669 survives. Under a wide, floppy felt hat he wears with apparent equanimity a thick horsehair wig which cascades well below his neck and conceals both ears. A long red coat, buttoned in front over the chest, reaches to the knees almost concealing plus fours apparently of the same material. Around his neck is a lace jabot, with more lace adorning the puffed bishop sleeves, the shoulders and the elbows. From each knee hang knots of ribbon and the stockings terminate in high-heeled shoes almost hidden by floppy bows. The Restoration fop, like his Regency buck great-grandson was, however, a very tough gentleman under his fine plumage and the short straight sword which hangs from a wide baldric over the right shoulder was no mere ornament.

The soldier's dress is listed in 'Sir Robert Harley's account for £2,000 paid for clothes for the Regiment of foot under his command at Tangier', now in the Public Record Office, showing '1,000 red coats at 13s 8d each; 200 white shirts at 3s 2d each; 1,000 pairs of breeches at 7s 10d per pair; 2,000 pairs of stockings at 1s 6d per pair; 2,000 pairs of shoes at 3s 3d per pair; 1,000 Monmouth caps at 2s 7d per cap'.

The Monmouth cap, a kind of tam o'shanter of which a specimen is preserved in Monmouth Museum, was the principal manufacture of the town in which it appeared to enjoy a monopoly.

Weapons for the foot were such as could be found in existing stores since there was no money available to buy better ones. Even as late as 1663 the Ordnance Minutes show that 1,000 pikes of thirteen foot length were being dispatched to the garrison although this piece of armoury had been generally discarded for all purposes elsewhere and its utility for defending trenches and redoubts against cavalry was questionable. The muskets were all, or nearly all, matchlocks; snaphaunces are not mentioned until several years later. The second-ary weapons were a curious assortment of ancient and modern. Large quantities of caltrops – small iron balls studded with spikes and used since the Dark Ages to deter cavalry – appear alongside numbers of hand grenades, which seem to have been used with better effect. Water bottles are nowhere mentioned although the absence of this essential piece of equipment had brought the army in Jamaica near to disaster in 1655. As leather was the one commodity easy to come by it is possible that they were produced locally. In this fashion the Tangier Regiments of horse and foot (more recently known as the First, the Royal Dragoons and the Queens, the Royal West Surreys[9]) were dis-patched to face an enemy hardly distinguishable from the one their ancestors with Coeur de Lion had fought and beaten at Arsuf.

Lord Sandwich had gone on ahead with 200 tons of stores to pre-pare for the arrival of the garrison and to sound out the nearest Moorish chieftain, Hamdi Ben Ali Gullah, commonly described as Gayland. To all appearances Gayland was not implacably hostile and he furnished a certain amount of forage and some slaughter cattle, though at a stiff price. While the regiments were mustering on Putney Heath, Sandwich was hard at work establishing commercial relations with the merchants of Cadiz for future supplies. The King of Spain had refused to recognise any transfer of sovereignty over Tangier, which from time to time he insisted against all evidence to be his, and Cadiz was in the lordship of Medina Sidonia. Despite the campaign in Portugal, however, there was no formal state of war and the Gaditanos were not averse from doing a lucrative business. In addition to this, the earl, an experienced seaman, spent much time in a small boat with lead-line and sounding-pole examining the likeli-est parts of Tangier Bay for a Mole. On one of these excursions he was nearly wrecked by a water-spout but he returned home with a

1. View of Tangier from the east.

good idea of the difficulties to be overcome. His fleet of eight fine ships, their gingerbread work shining in the African sun, furnished sufficient seaman gunners to man the defences as the Portuguese marched out leaving behind only one troop of cavalry. These, for some reason known only to themselves, made a raid into the countryside on 14 January 1662 and carried off 400 head of cattle; on the return journey the Moors were waiting for them under cover of the sand-hills. The Portugal horse were routed and fled to the safety of the walls and the Royal Navy. Sandwich was furious, but the damage was done. Thus matters stood when, on 29 January, the topsails of Lord Peterborough's ships were descried from the castle and within a matter of hours his advance parties began to disembark on the open beach. On the whole the incident probably did as much good as harm. Don Francisco de Almeida, the Portuguese governor, was known to be furiously resentful of the order that he hand over a Portuguese possession to heretics. The governor of Bombay had refused to do so and Don Francisco might have been tempted to do the same but for the necessity under which he now found himself. The decencies were observed and sovereignty transferred.

Christendom in North Africa, all four acres of it, continued precariously to exist. The army, now recognisable as such, set to work learning to make war upon an irregular enemy since the lessons it had learned in formal war either at home or on the continent were of little value here. It was a prelude to coming centuries in which its successors would have to take on not merely the armies of France but the deadlier, if less organised, hordes of Afghans, Dervishes, Zulus and assorted tribesmen of the North-West Frontier of India. Neither Marston Moor nor Breitenfeld had taught how best to cope with the swarms of horsemen whose ancestors had followed Saladin and furnished England with so many Moor's or Saracen's Heads. Nor had conventional warfare taught them much about the other Moorish speciality, the ambush and counter-ambush. As it would have to do time and again in the future the army devised new battle-drills suitable for the conditions in which it found itself. Chindits, Commandos and SAS might all fairly claim some sort of descent from the Tangier garrison.

Shortage of men could not be made good by superior weapons. The pike, until as late as 1702, was the infantryman's backbone. In the open, as a defence against cavalry, there was something to be said for it but elsewhere it could have been no more than a nuisance. Officers, though theoretically equipped with eight-foot-long spontoons, usually carried pistols in addition. The musketeers were armed with left-overs from the Civil War, both matchlock and snaphaunces still being in service; book 47 of the War Office and Ordnance Papers shows that in 1680 the Tangier garrison was sent 1,000 of the former and 700 of the latter. There is no earlier figure given. The musketeer carried a short sword. King Charles had experimented with the bayonet but had not made much progress. Soon after the Restoration he had obtained from King Louis 500 of the earliest bayonets, the plug variety. It was a kind of hunting knife with a round handle that could be jammed into the muzzle, turning the musket into a spear; for the moment it was probably better than nothing but the musket barrels were more serviceable than an iron-shod butt, which did not put in an appearance until after the Tangier episode was over. Neither kind of musket was at its best in the wet. Nor was the other infantryman's stand-by. One of the favourite songs of the day, if the Roxburghe Ballads are to be believed begins with 'Captain Hume is bound to sea' and finishes with 'When we come to Tangier's shore, we'll make our grenades to roar'. They might well have done so, but with difficulty in the rain. Mr Bonsal, whom you may remember as spending his honeymoon there, wrote that

> Tangier is a charming winter resort, but I have often wondered why it is not frequented in larger numbers by ducks. The weather during the winter solstice is certainly very suitable for the web-footed. It is true that it does not rain all the winter, but when it does rain it rains for weeks at a time. Tangier's really a summer city. From April until November the weather is delightful.

There was also the wind. When HMS *Scout* visited the place in 1853 – of which more later – her captain wrote of it with some feeling.

> In all the directions given for this bay no mention whatsoever is made of the NW wind, the Easterly being considered the worst which certainly is most frequent and brings with it a swell into the Bay but it must be nothing compared to a North Westerly gale blowing direct inshore and having a stretch of open land for thousands of miles. During our short stay here it was only a fresh breeze from that quarter but the swell that sets into the Bay in the course of an hour is scarcely credible.

Spare a thought for English matchlock men on the walls trying to load and fire in these less than perfect conditions.

2

Vacant Possession

It would not be true to say that the acquisition of the city of Tangier had been greeted with full-hearted enthusiasm in England. The House of Commons, beset by financial difficulties, grudged every penny laid out on the business and had no confidence in its future prosperity as a free port. The King, the Duke of York and the best brains in the country, however, took a different view, inclining to that of Sir Robert Southwell that it would make England 'master of the trade in the Mediterranean'. The Royal Navy was still the navy of Robert Blake and his contemporaries, entirely equal to the task if it were capable of being performed at all. James, Duke of York was a competent Lord High Admiral and he had the advantage of being advised by that man of many talents, Rupert of the Palatinate, Duke of Cumberland. The combination of Rupert, whose privateering fleet had been defeated by Blake off Cartagena a dozen years before and the Cromwellian Admiral Montagu, worked well.

Peterborough, whose nephew was to become the eccentric but successful commander of the British forces in Spain during a great war and who was aboard one of the transports as a colonel of the horse, has left little in the way of personal remembrance. It is, however, certain that he was a close friend to James and a man well fitted for his present appointment. The wounds of the Civil War do not seem to have been deep in the sea service, for Peterborough and Sandwich were on terms of cordiality and assisted each other to the full extent of their powers.

The fourteen-day voyage from the Downs was a prosperous one, so far as travel in small, crowded sailing ships could ever deserve that traditional adjective. No vessel was lost, the bay was crossed without excessive discomfort and recent memories of Kentish fields under snow soon disappeared as Englishmen discovered that the sun was a phenomenon which they hardly understood. Mantled in sweat under their heavy clothing and shielding screwed up eyes with their hands they crowded the bulwarks to watch the slowly approaching shores of Africa, the first of so many generations of British soldiers to undergo an experience that few men ever quite forget. The light, scented breeze carried towards them the faint popping of musketry as the Portugal horse fled for the safety of the city walls. Before the last anchor had splashed down into a sea of incredible blue a deputation was alongside the flagship urgently requesting immediate help. Forty men each from the *Royal James* and the *Princess* were swiftly embarked in ships' boats and rowed ashore to help out the sailors who were manning the Portuguese cannon, a further 120 followed on the next day and by 23 January 1662 the first 400 were ashore under command of Sir Richard Stayner. By nightfall he was able to report that he was in possession of the castle and all the magazines and strong points.

The men left in the ships had leisure to examine the prospect before them. The dominant colour was a kind of sepia, the hills on which the city was built and the rolling sand-hills around and beyond it offering no contrast. Only inside the walls, rising up in terraces, from the water's edge, was there an occasional flash of cool green from the little gardens that had been so lovingly tended by their departed owners over the last two centuries. At first glance it did not seem that lack of water was likely to be one of their difficulties. Nobody could be expected to realise that this state of affairs was not going to continue. The Portuguese over several generations had worked out an elaborate system of irrigation. Samuel Pepys described it many years later: 'This place was the fullest in the world, every house having a particular well or two, now dry and lost by losing the knowledge whither to go to the conduit head to remedy it'. A detailed knowledge of the water system would have been so valuable to a besieger that only one description of it was kept, in a book strictly reserved for the use of the governor and nobody else. The book was handed by the outgoing incumbent to Lord Peterborough with strong advice to insist, as his predecessors had done, that none but he be allowed ever to see it. Lord Peterborough followed this wise counsel to the letter. When he left Tangier in May 1662 the book went with him and was never seen again. Its existence was known and when its return was requested Peterborough replied lightly that he could not find it. For the moment, however, water was plentiful. More worrying to the experienced soldiers was the fact that the city was on all sides, bar the sea, overlooked by hills that seemed empty but most certainly were not. It was a little worrying, but if the Portuguese, who were not as highly regarded as soldiers as they were as seamen, could hold the place it should not be too difficult for the King's red-coats.

Peterborough's instructions about the use of what the city had to give were clear.

> As for the houses, having first provided for the convenient lodging of the garrison you shall dispose of the rest to merchants according to your liking either by reserving good rents upon them or otherwise taking fines... excepting only such houses as were effectually bought by the Earl of Sandwich and some few other officers of the Fleet.

Those abandoned by the Portuguese were to be fairly valued and paid for. Officers who had the money soon bought themselves little whitewashed Moorish houses with their pleasant gardens and their trees of fig and orange. The bulk of the garrison did not do so well and the deficiencies soon manifested themselves. Peterborough summoned a council of war, made up of the eight field officers in the garrison, which met in the castle on 12 February 1662. Its conclusions were embodied in a long report which was despatched to Whitehall the same day. The garrison now numbered 3,218 all ranks; their pay was already three months in arrears. Wheat and oil were running short but these could be bought in Cadiz where both were far cheaper and of better quality than in England. Fuel for cooking was almost non-existent, for there was no wood to be had and 1,500 cauldrons of coal were a pressing necessity together with 600 iron cooking pots. A request for 2,000 beds – an unusual luxury – was followed by dark hints that if these things were not provided there would be sickness which would 'destroy the garrison and affright all people coming hither to traffic and commerce, the inhabitants who were here all removing leaving only bare walls'. Having dealt with the essentials for maintaining life, the dispatch spoke of war material: 'The guns being the greatest part dismounted and the rest with carriages unfit for service... in general the place is very little more than a ruin of walls'. The document was signed by all present including Nathaniel Luke, the governor's secretary. It was fortunate for the garrison that there was no attack during the early months for the Portuguese guns were useless and there were no works to prevent an enemy marching by night up to the crumbling walls which were the first and last defence. Though it soon became plain that, in the old North-West Frontier expression, the eye of the tribesman was always watching them, the garrison units were able to shake themselves down without molestation. The reason was not that the Moors intended to accept their intrusive presence but simply that Ali Gayland was engaged in a private war with his cousin Ben Barka, ruler of the pirate port of Sallee. This happy state of affairs was not likely to endure for long and Peterborough sent letters to Gayland by the first possible messenger to ask for a meeting at which some *modus vivendi* might be arranged. In the meantime the troops were put to work botching up the old defences as best they could and the first merchants began to arrive. 'The Company of Royal Adventurers of England trading in Africa' had been set up by charter and Tangier was a useful halting place on the way to its main place of interest, the Gambia River that Rupert had learnt to know during his exile. Others arrived also to take up residence in the empty houses with an eye to commercial activities nearer at hand; expansion of trade was in the air and the City of London was never averse to stealing a march on its Dutch rivals.

On 24 March 1662 letters from Gayland came into the city; he was prepared to meet the Christian leader and, seemingly, to come to some sort of arrangement. A place was agreed, well outside the walls, and there a couple of days later the strange rendezvous was kept. For the first time since the Crusades pink-cheeked Englishmen and dark, Moorish warriors met to take stock of each other and to talk of peace. Peterborough and his escort of cavalry, heavy horse with helmets and straight sabres, trotted out to meet the Arab cavalry, robed in violet and white and armed with curved swords of wicked sharpness. The English were favourably impressed. 'Their army which appeared here were about 5,000 horse, able, dexterous, sober, valiant, incomparably well armed and clothed', wrote Peterborough, asserting firmly that they were the best cavalry he had ever seen. The Dragoons, it is fair to speculate, were less impressed by circus tricks but wondered how such fellows would stand in a knee-to-knee charge. Gayland was affable enough, though he made it plain that he should not be counted Peterborough's friend nor taken as acquiescing in Roumi possession of a single feddan of Arab land. For the moment, however, there need not be war between them, though Peterborough must buy his peace at Gayland's price. It would, for a start, be a modest one for a six-month armistice. Let fifty barrels of powder be sent to the Moorish camp and let a promise be given that all intercourse with his enemies at Tetuan should cease, and the English would remain for that time untroubled. Peterborough, having little choice, agreed. The powder would have to come from London, though he did not find it necessary to say that he could not spare it from his own stocks; the break with Tetuan ('Titvan' he called it) was a nuisance, for it possessed a consul and beef could be bought there, but it would be worth it. Moorish alliances shifted so quickly that it would probably not be for long. The perspiring red-coats rode back with an agreement. 'We thought fit to conclude a peace for six months were it but to begin the way of trade', the governor wrote home,

> and to show the Moors by practice with us that we were
> men of such manners and dealing as might procure a love

and confidence at last… It must be great fear, or an exceeding interest, that brings them to be so kind to any stranger
especially to a Christian. Jealous they are beyond all measure of their land.

The letter ends with a further, almost despairing, request for fuel.
Amongst the Tangier State Papers there remains a bill of freight
dated 26 August for '50 chaldrons of New Cassel coale', a substantial reduction on the 1,500 demanded. Winter nights in Tangier are
cold and the wind is a standing reminder that this is an Atlantic seaport as well as an African town. Curious the Moors undoubtedly
were, but fear had no part in their behaviour. On 3 May 1662, well
before the truce had expired, the two sides met in arms. The fight,
of which details are scanty, began when a large body of Moorish
cavalry appeared unheralded under the walls. All the evidence suggests that this was no chance-medley but a well-laid plan of a kind
regularly employed by Islamic armies from time immemorial. The
'feigned flight', usually a very successful ploy, had been standard
practice against the Crusaders centuries earlier; it was, indeed, the
specialité de la maison of Nur-ed-Din of Syria who had destroyed
more than one Christian army, including that of Baldwin of
Jerusalem at the Horns of Hattin in 1187. It is understandable that
English officers might have forgotten these things, and even how
the battle of Hastings had been lost in much the same way, but Arab
memories are longer. Lieutenant-Colonel Fiennes, seeing it as no
more than a piece of insolence deserving sharp punishment,
quickly collected together some 500 men and marched them out
through the main gate to repel the invaders.

The red-coats tore into the Arab horsemen with a splendid dash
and drove them off in confusion. Fiennes, believing himself to have
won a demonstrable victory and anxious to complete it, carried on
his pursuit into the desert until his men were on the point of
exhaustion and he was obliged to turn about. As they made their
way wearily back under an African sun further bodies of Moorish
cavalry appeared from their lurking places amongst the sand-hills

and charged the little force from several directions. The matchlock musket without bayonet was a poor weapon for such work, and the English soldiers could do no more than straggle back to safety as best they could. Of the original force nearly a half, 246 men, were killed or disappeared. Rumours came back of the fate of some prisoners, who had either been tortured to death or walled up alive. It was an expensive and painful introduction into desert warfare. It was also, perhaps, prophetic that the first fight of the regular army in its first campaign should end in defeat. The city was in no real danger for even the Portuguese museum-piece guns were sufficient to keep the Moors at a distance. They did, however, continue to raid up to the walls from time to time and carried off whatever cattle they could find. The garrison recovered from the shock and began once more to patrol outside the walls while the new field works were being built. A timely draft for £12,000, part of Queen Catharine's dowry, brought their pay nearly up to date.

It became plain early on that a city could not exist forever in a state of siege without any knowledge of what its enemy was about and it was soon after the May battle that the first English intelligence officer amongst the Arabs assumed his duties. In recent years many such, of whom the names of Kitchener, Reginald Wingate and T.E. Lawrence come most readily to mind, have shown remarkable aptitude for so unlikely a mission but of the first man to go out into the desert amongst an alien people and to learn their ways little trace remains. Amongst the Tangier Papers for 1662 repose a number of reports of Moorish feuds and intentions over the signature of James Wilson. In June 1662 he reported that Gayland, who had been laying siege to Ben Barka in Tetuan, had settled the quarrel and was going to Fez with the object of making himself Emperor. How Wilson came by his information can now never be known but he was correct in every detail. Tangier was granted a breathing space and Lord Peterborough went home, taking the waterworks manual with him. Gayland sent in his emissaries to negotiate for peace but they were coldly received. Wilson had done his work well, for the deputy governor was entirely aware not only that Gayland needed peace in order to free his hands up for other business but also that he had been colluding with the Duke of Medina Sidonia to cut off supplies to the city. Gayland had met with no success in that quarter, not because the duke was unwilling but because the Spanish merchants refused to give up a valuable trade. The garrison had 'boats in plenty and want no refreshment, beef excepted'. As there was nothing to be gained from an agreement with a chief whose undertakings were demonstrably worthless the envoys were sent home without any serious negotiation taking place.

The summer passed without any fighting save for a few small chance-medleys of little importance. The over-riding consideration, after the landward fortifications, was the building of a mole and the first plans were produced during these months. On 31 October 1662 an estimate for a bridge stretching out to sea for 100 yards and with a width of twenty yards was drawn up and submitted by Jonathan Shish and a Mr Rimbetts. The price quoted was £572 10s, which seems reasonable enough, but the plan was not accepted. That well-informed man John Evelyn knew 'old shish' well and has much to say about him in his diary. Shish was a wonderful shipwright of the old school, practically illiterate but responsible for the fine vessels that Deptford yard had sent to serve with the fleet. In a venal age he did not make a vice of incorruptibility and, in any event, this was work for an engineer of another kind. Three weeks later, on 20 November 1662, a further royal warrant established Tangier as a free port under the commissioners, of whom the most important were the Duke of York, Rupert, Monck (now Duke of Albemarle), Sandwich and Peterborough. The first year's expenses had been far greater than expected, with bills totalling only a few pounds short of £70,000, but it did look as if the city and port of Tangier was indeed going to be a valuable long-term investment for the Crown and people.

3
Disputed Title

It is said that an old Arab proverb asserts a lie to be excusable in three circumstances: in war, to reconcile friends, and to a woman. Gayland, like all good Muslims, adhered firmly to the view that no peace between Islam and the hated Nazrani was ever possible and, in consequence, no treaty needed to be kept longer than his purpose required.[9] This cut both ways. As soon as his lack of faith in making war during a time of truce became apparent, the English seized upon it as a breach which discharged the contract and entitled them to do as they pleased. The reply to the Moorish adage lay in the English legal maxim that '*salus populi suprema lex est*' and safety could not be assured so long as the power of the new owners extended no further than the footings of the curtain wall. Almost at once the garrison engineers were put to work preparing plans for extra-mural fortifications and soon fatigue parties were hard at it with mattock and shovel under an African sun.

The beginnings were simple enough under the limitations of the materials that could be had on the spot. First, a single line of trench was spitlocked out within musket shot of the wall; this was no mere slit in the ground but a great anti-cavalry obstacle twenty-four feet across at its widest and with a depth varying between fifteen and eighteen feet. A line of palisades, thickened out with Swedish feathers (sharpened stakes dug in at an angle) and well sprinkled with caltrops was erected in front of the most vulnerable places and on the left of the position, the south side, earthworks of a solid kind were thrown up. The castle, now called York Castle, was refurbished as far as resources allowed but its state was not far removed from ruinous. Happily its position at the north-east corner and close to the sea was not much exposed and it served well enough as a head-quarters for the governor. More important was the Upper Castle which formed a garth on the angle where the north and west walls joined. The remains of an old tower were taken in hand and built up to a height from which a sentry could see well over the sand-hills.

Lord Peterborough himself returned home in May 1662 leaving the command in the hands of his deputy, Colonel Fitzgerald. It appears that he must have had a private understanding with the King and the Duke of York that he would only remain so long as was necessary to get the affairs of Tangier on a proper footing, for he was an important figure about the Court and could not be expected to endure protracted exile. His duties had been carried out faithfully, apart from the matter of the water supply book, for the Tangier State Papers speak of him as having 'paid off all arrears and filled up all stores and ammunitions' as well as having 'opened up a good understanding with Algiers and with Sallee. The works were strengthened by the same noble lord; the garrison enlarged, the quarters were disposed, the rate of victuals settled; the guards were ordered, and five miles round clearly gained'. One should not grudge him the life pension of £1,000 per annum that he was awarded on his return.

It was during Peterborough's absence, however, that fighting flared up again. Hardly any details have come down to us beyond a few general observations but the muster rolls speak for themselves. Between Peterborough's departure in May and his return in October the Governor's Regiment lost nearly 200 men and that of Sir Robert Harley a little under 400 men. As the other two, smaller, regiments maintained a consistent strength it is fair to assume that these were battle casualties and not the result of some epidemic. The Moors were said to have lost more than 500 men, the brother of Gayland being amongst the dead. Fitzgerald obviously won a considerable reputation, for the Tangier Council is reported as having wished to see him confirmed as Peterborough's successor. The appointment, however, went elsewhere, apparently because

Fitzgerald was an Irish Catholic and the King was sensitive about accusations of favouritism in that direction. The place went instead to Lord Rutherford, soon to be Earl of Teviot, who was of the same religion but not an Irishman. Samuel Pepys wrote in his diary that 'I am sorry to see a Catholic Governor sent to command there where all the rest of the officers almost are such already'. This was probably an exaggeration, but the appointment contained the seeds of future trouble. Even so, it was understandable. The governor of Tangier would necessarily have much to do with Spanish and Portuguese grandees to whom a heretic was hardly more tolerable than a heathen Moor.

Teviot does not seem to have been much liked. Lord Sandwich feared that 'from the few friends he hath left, and the ill posture of his affairs, my Lord Teviot is not a man for the conduct and management that people take him to be'. His last task had been to lower the flag at Dunkirk and to hand that hard-won place over to the French and such duties do not make for popularity. Nevertheless all Lord Teviot's future actions go to show that he was a good soldier and a man of much personal courage. His commission is dated 9 April 1663 and on 28 April he was writing from Deal to his friend Mr Williamson (Bennett's private secretary) that he is on his way to Tangier with some soldiers and is only waiting for a fair wind. This was not his only contribution to the garrison for, again according to Pepys, 'he had laid out some seven or eight thousand pounds in commodities for the place'.

Teviot arrived some time in May 1663 and walked straight into a battle. A small redoubt was being built to hold 100 men and six guns, 'on the top of the hill which overlooketh the town to the very ports thereof'. This was too much for Gayland, who made preparations for an attack. On 4 June Teviot wrote to Mr Secretary Bennett that 'These three days past we have been under arms, as we are informed by fugitives from him that he has 4,000 horse and 2,000 foot to attack our little new Fort, and at this instant I expect him sallying on us'. For ten days the trenches were manned by the entire garrison fit for duty some 1,200 infantry divided into three groups and ninety troopers of the Tangier horse in reserve. The line stretched from the sea on the south east to a point on the little stream that runs through the town about half a mile outside the western wall; so well had Peterborough left the magazines stocked that 36,000 caltrops were scattered in the likely ways of approach, together with a few crude land-mines. Three Moorish regiments, 'one in red and white, another in black and the third in a sort of violet colour', the second led by Gayland himself, appeared early on the morning of 14 June and seem to have caught the defenders by surprise. Most of them abandoned the trenches in what seems indecent haste but the situation was saved by Major Rudyard and some thirty or forty men in the new fort. These brave men refused to budge and kept up a steady fire with their matchlocks and grenades as the Moorish horse concentrated around their position. After half an hour of hard fighting, during which two-thirds of them were killed or wounded, they were relieved by a dashing charge of the reserve of the Tangier horse from the town, led by Colonel Tobias Bridges who had made a name for himself in Tobago. Bridges, with his handful of dragoons, swept the Moorish cavalry away before him and the foot resumed the posts they had abandoned. Teviot sent a rebuke to Gayland by the hand of two Jews reproaching him for so rude a welcome. Gayland returned a courteous reply, in Spanish, thanked Teviot for his offer to return the Moorish dead and even sent back a stray prisoner who had fallen into his hands some days before. A correspondence followed which surely reminded some of Coeur de Lion and Saladin for its polite irony. It ended, early in August, with an agreement for a further truce for six months.

This time it was the English who broke the agreement. Teviot, without any claim of right, promptly engrossed a further 1,000 acres or so of Moorish land to extend the glacis of his city. On it he set his men to work erecting a substantial redoubt, named Fort Charles, some three furlongs outside the walls to the south west with a covered way leading from it through the wall by Peterborough Tower. Another, smaller, fort named Pole's Redoubt (almost certainly the 'new little fort' of the last battle), was begun at the same time, covering the Catherine Port at the other end of the long west wall and at about the same distance in front of it. Both stood behind the trench line, inside which the garrison's cattle could now graze in safety.

Gayland did not accept these intrusions with equanimity. On 1 May 1663 the sentry on Peterborough Tower observed considerable activity around Pole's Redoubt and it soon became clear that the Moors were preparing to attack the still uncompleted work. This was the chance the garrison had long awaited. The Tangier horse formed up inside the Catherine Port in a solid block while the foot ran on to the ramparts to watch the fight. Teviot personally ordered Captain Witham to bring back the red flag flying over the Moorish position, the gate was flung open and the horse roared out in the first knee-to-knee charge since Naseby. Colonel Walton would surely permit repetition of his account of what happened.

> On those sunny slopes in front of the walls of Tangier promise was given of the troopers that should capture French colours at Waterloo and ride through Russian masses at Balaklava. A most dashing onset, afterwards maintained with greatest spirit, placed the standard in the hands of English troopers and effectually routed the enemy.

The Moors were excellent light horsemen but the weight and shock of a charge by heavy cavalry had not been experienced since the last fights, long ago, with the mailed chivalry of Spain and it was something against which they could not stand. For some time the garrison was left unmolested and the work went on, save only for a brief interruption a fortnight later when other Moorish troops from Meknes decided to show their vanquished countrymen that they were at least a match for any Roumi. The result was the same and the Royals, to give them their familiar name, once more thundered massively down on their enemies and routed them. The defeats gave the Moors food for thought. Their fashion of war limited itself to the cloud of horsemen swamping an enemy in the field and to the ambush usually following a pretended rout. The former style was plainly going to need much change, though the latter could continue forever as opportunities came. It would, however, be necessary to study the attack on defended places and for this they were not yet equipped. Guns and gunners, sappers and miners would all be needed and they had none, though there were always the Spaniards who might be willing to help old enemies against new ones. Gayland addressed himself to sounding them out.

Lord Teviot also had a dominating factor in his scheme of things. Until the Mole existed in some form Tangier was less a port than a prison. The commissioners met to discuss plans on 3 April 1663. Samuel Pepys, informed presumably by his friend Lord Sandwich, wrote glumly about its conclusions.

> We find ourselves at a great stand, the establishment being but £70,000 per annum, and the forces to be kept in the town at the least estimate that my Lord Rutherford can be got to bring is £53,000. The charge of this year's work in the Mole will be £13,000 besides £1,000 a year to my Lord Peterborough as a pension and the fortifications and contingencies, which puts us to a great stand.

Great stand or no, the work had to be carried out or the city might as well be abandoned. On 20 November 1662 a commission was given to James, Duke of York to see that it was done. Whatever his defects as a monarch, James was a sensible and practical man. His plan was an ambitious one, far in advance of anything done since Rome declined and fell, and his first charge was to find the men capable of turning it into reality. There was, luckily, some sort of precedent. Sir Hugh Cholmley, of Whitby in the county of Yorkshire, had had recent experience in building a pier there which, though puny beside the work now contemplated, had coped with much the same difficulties. Sir Hugh (who succeeded to his father's baronetcy in 1665) explained it all in a pamphlet, and he was frank about the errors that had been made. The Whitby Mole was begun by pitching huge stones into the sea for a distance of 200 yards, they having been then 'bound with great pieces of wood let into the foundation and cross-bound with others let into the stone, and bolted with iron'. The North Sea had made short work of this. Cholmley, brooding by the water's edge on the reasons for his failure, noticed idly that a small tree set up as a sea-mark for shipping seemed to have come through the same storms without any trouble. From this he drew the conclusion that

> the cause was that the sea had a free passage about the tree, and that though they might and would not stand if set contiguously, yet if placed in several rows they abated or intercepted the weight of the seas and so protected the principal work, viz. the pier or Mole.

Thus inspired, he made enquiries about the Mole at Genoa, where even the tideless Mediterranean had smashed massive hard stones 'laid in lime and tarrace [cement] so that it seems an entire rock near twenty yards thick'. When the Genoese engineers had reinforced it with an outpost line of large rocks carefully positioned to take the first shock of the waves the Genoa Mole had stood up successfully. It had, in its final shape, been built up from a series of 'chests, 54 feet long (that being the width of the Mole) by 36 in breadth and 18 in depth'. The chests had been floated over a mass of loose stones, filled in with rock and rubble until they sank and then welded together with cement. What had worked at Genoa ought, with luck, to work at Tangier. Even if no luck was to be expected nobody could think of a better way of going about the task.

Cholmley, having been contracted to build a mole at 13s a cubic yard, arrived at Tangier on 1 June 1663 accompanied by 'about 40 masons, miners and other artists and workmen'. It seems that recruiting had not been easy, for Tangier had a bad name as the result of some highly-coloured accounts of the hardships which the first arrivals had undergone. In sober truth Tangier was always a healthy station once one had become used to short commons when the storms blew up or Spanish or Dutch warships disrupted supplies. The most common ailments were malaria and dysentery. Mosquitoes abounded – mosquito nets are often mentioned – but nobody saw them as having anything to do with the fever and the Jesuits' Bark – quinine – was not discovered until just before the place was evacuated.

The first three months were taken up with interior economy, including the building of a separate village, Whitby, on the sea shore about half a mile west of the walls. There it was at least shielded from that curse of the builders, the wind called Levanter. Work on the Mole began in August and appeared promising. In the following February, however, Cholmley was summoned home for urgent family reasons and was away for the rest of the year. By the time he came back the work force had grown to nearly 200 tradesmen of all kinds but the good progress had not been kept up. Far too often the molemen had had to down tools and either repair the forts or serve as soldiers. Whitby, however, had been made independent of the garrison in terms of stores and it contained rations enough to keep the men supplied for nearly a twelvemonth. The main building was a barrack block 240 feet long by fifteen feet wide, according to the book of Tangier plans in Windsor Castle. The difficulty, Cholmley was told, was moving the stone from the quarry which was outside the village to the Mole, for the lighters were constantly driven back by the Levanter. Cholmley, who seems to have earned his baronetcy, obtained wood from somewhere, built carts and imported about ninety horses from Spain. After that work progressed more quickly and by the end of the year Cholmley was able to return home for good leaving the work in the hands of Mr Shere. In January 1665 'the part that is now above the ground at this time' amounted to

10,558 cubic yards. A year later the Mole was big enough and strong enough to bear a battery of guns which was of great service in beating off an attack on Tangier by a Dutch fleet. The King agreed to add 4s a cubic yard to the price agreed with the commissioners but it does not appear that Sir Hugh ended with much to show for his hard work . The 1668 plan shows one of the first buildings to have gone up on the Mole as a tavern which perhaps brought him some small revenue. At all events, it must have been welcome to the men of Whitby.

4
Lord Teviot

Though the dash and skill of the Tangier horse had won a breathing space for the garrison, the enemies of King Charles and his city of Tangier were gathering. Gayland's intrigues with Spain were nothing new but, so far, little had happened to show him any advantage from them. Even before Lord Teviot had arrived, Colonel Fitzgerald had reported to Mr Secretary Bennett (the future Lord Arlington) the arrival of a Spanish delegation bearing a present 'worth more than forty thousand pieces of eight' and some hard information had been obtained. Late in November 1663 an English friar had turned up at Tangier for no obvious reason. Major Knightly 'made it his business to sift this friar', one of his lesser aids to ascertaining the truth being to tell the man that it was disgraceful for Christians to join with the Moors to fight against other Christians. The friar replied that 'they would join with the Devil to have Tangier'. The Duke of Medina Sidonia would have considered this hyperbole, but he had no reason to feel well disposed towards England. Seville, in his duchy, was the centre of affairs for Spanish America and reports of buccaneer outrage reached him with monotonous regularity. The Revd Lancelot Addison, who appears to have witnessed the reception of the Spanish Mission at Tetuan by Gayland, wrote of the matter in his 'Short Narrative of the Revolutions in the Kingdoms of Fez and Morocco' saying that the

> Duke had an evil eye upon the immortal Teviot for the
> renowned victories which, under the most Christian King,

he achieved against his nation's interest in the Low Countries, which aged choler he found highly inflamed by the victories gained by that indefatigable Captain over his Moresco neighbours.

Gayland, with the most disarming air imaginable, presented himself under the walls shortly afterwards and, at his invitation, the deputy governor went hawking with his deadly enemy in the open country.

It was not only Spain, however, that seemed about to enter the lists. If amity between the Moors and the sons of El Cid Campeador seemed against nature even more so was one between Hollanders and the sons of the men who had helped Alva to burn and kill throughout the Seven Provinces.

There arose, however, a common interest when, in the early summer of 1664, the sporadic sea-fights that were taking place between the Gambia River and the Suffolk coast blazed into open war between England and Holland.

The direct impact on Tangier was not great, a Dutch squadron being driven off by English guns and the infant Mole proving its usefulness by giving shelter to the Newfoundland fleet, but the indirect results were serious. The Royal Navy had its hands full fighting it out with Opdam in battles where Rupert and Monck were to demonstrate how well thoughtful soldiers could command fleets. Convoys became fewer and smaller and money, the essential stuff of war as much as of commerce, ceased to arrive at all.

It was fortunate for the garrison that the March battles happened when they did. Teviot, who lived in the field as hard as any private soldier, had a reputation for invincibility. Mr Addison wrote to his friend Williamson that 'The Moors call him Devil. They report that he never sleeps, that his great guns run out of themselves and that he is a man of success and cannot be beaten'. Gayland found it prudent to allow his people to bring in cattle and forage against payment in cash or kind. Redoubts continued to be traced out, more trenches dug and the infantry element was re-organised. The two strong and two weak battalions were re-formed as two regiments, the English

2. A view of Tangier looking towards the sandhills.

regiment of fifteen companies and the Irish of five. This arrangement does not seem to have endured for long as references soon appear to the Old Tangier Regiment, plainly an amalgamation of both. Twice during March Gayland tried to ambush them as they covered the building of Fort Charles and twice he was driven away without loss to our side. It was satisfactory but it is never wise to underrate an enemy who has the driving force of religion behind him.

Nemesis, as usual, followed close behind hubris. The King was the first to learn of it when a letter was delivered bearing on its back the urgent words 'May 5th '64. Sir Tob. Bridges to His Maty. FOR THE KINGE'. It told how Lord Teviot had acquired such an ascendancy over the Moors that they had for some time past only shown their faces in small numbers at a respectful distance and for the last few days not at all.

> This gave encouragement to My Lord to march over the Jews River up into a thick bushy wood, opposite to the hill on the westward sea, and went there with a party of foot over three miles without any resistance made where they found only one house built with stone and lime, the which was by them quit upon My Lord's approach... Upon the 3rd of this instant, my Lord having made early in the morning a further

discovery with his horse than ever he had done at any time before to the south-east, and having placed sentinels and guards, judging the country for a great distance at least to be clear of any enemy, ordained all the horse to forage there, directing some foot to lie near them for making good the retreat if anything should happen; and he himself took a resolution to go into the wood with some foot to cut wood, and immediately went over the valley to the west hill towards Fort Charles and took with him seven battalions of foot, all firelocks, the best and choicest of our men, and the principal and chief officers of the garrison to command them; he himself being accompanied with several gentlemen volunteers and reformed officers marched over the Jews River into the wood and went up three several ways, they being all appointed to meet at some particular place some distance above the hill. But it was notwithstanding his far discovery before made by the horse, which I fear produced more than ordinary confidence; before they came up to the middle party of the hill in the wood, several ambushes of foot discovered themselves with which our men skirmished and drove to a retreat but presently on all hands they rose up and appeared in such great numbers that they immediately had surrounded our men, at the same time the horse started up round about in the valley and on the hills to the south-east not less than two thousand and came pouring down not only upon our horse but took the advantage in a moment to fall between the wood where our foot were and the hill, that although it was evident that our men fought as resolutely and gave as good fire as men could do, they being thus surrounded with their army of horse and foot. Our worthy General, the officers and gentlemen with him, and all the whole party of the soldiers, were cut off, not thirty of them, as I can find, that ever came off. There is lost in this action His Excellency The Earl of Teviot, our General, with nineteen commissioned officers, and fifteen gentlemen and volun-

teers, the doctor, together with 396 non-commissioned officers and private soldiers, the particular of which and other
things is sent to Mr Secretary. This sad misfortune and great
breach hath filled us all with sorrow and distraction, yet are
all willing to contribute our utmost for the safety of this
place and, if possible, to preserve those forts which already
hath cost so much care and charges. The officers remaining
have with joint consent been pleased to command me at
present to manage the garrison concerns, which I shall with
all faith and loyalty endeavour to discharge according to my
capacity until Your Majesty's pleasure be known. I have taken
a view of both regiments of foot and find present but four
Captains, the one of namely Captain Mordaunt is very sick
and unserviceable at present, very few Lieutenants and
Ensigns, and these not of the best, some companies not any
commissioned officers left, which hath necessitated me, in
order to the discharge of our duty, to elect such persons
amongst ourselves as were judged the most sufficient to act as
officers for the present until Your Majesty's further order.

In a separate note Bridges informed the King that he reckoned to
have five weeks rations and plenty of ammunition but the desperate need was for men, firelocks and tools. Lime was badly needed to
finish Fort Charles as the Spaniards had hanged all the men they
had caught trying to buy it from Cadiz. The note is far from hyster-
ical – Bridges was not that kind of man – but says quietly that
while, for want of men, he doubts whether he can hold the forts
against a serious attack, they can always be built again. Pay, he men-
tions, is more than six months in arrears and would be welcome.
Lastly there is a message for Fitzgerald, the deputy governor, who
happened to be on leave: will he please make it his business to send
to Lady Teviot, who was in France, and stop her from finishing her
journey to Tangier.

The only eye-witness account of Teviot's last fight came from
one of his servants who contrived to get away. His tale, which

could never be verified, was that the governor with some 400 or 500 men had been attacked by about 3,000 horse and had driven them off, apparently routed. Following on their heels for about a quarter of a mile the English marched – or were drawn – on to the main ambush of ten times their number. Teviot managed to carve his way to a hillock called the Jews' Mount and there, back to back, the Tangier Regiment fought it out, pike and clubbed musket against sword and lance, with no quarter asked or given. In all only nine men came back; the survivors believed the English to have killed three for one in their death struggle and they may well have been right. It is certain that no attack was made on Bridges' remnant and not a position was lost. Teviot, though a newcomer to Tangier, should have known better than to fall into such a trap but the manner of their fight to the death has never been surpassed even in the long history of the Queen's regiment. What happened to the horse is not clear, for no cavalry officers are listed amongst the casualties. The probability is that Teviot took with him no more than a small scouting party and that they died fighting with the others. The only crumb of comfort left for Bridges was that none of the gunners had taken part in Teviot's foray and the sovereign weapon of the defence was unimpaired; the matchlock musket was a miserable affair but the artillery pieces, many of them newly supplied by the navy to replace the worn out objects left by the Portuguese, were as good as anything the army was to possess for the next couple of centuries. His other asset was the plentiful supply of grenades[10]. This most useful ancillary was well understood and carefully studied as a late seventeenth-century battle-winner; the iron sphere about the size of a cricket ball, stuffed with powder and scrap-iron and ignited by a length of match was a far more efficient tool than the makeshifts supplied to the army of 1915. The Royal Society itself did not disdain experiments to improve the weapon. John Evelyn's diary entry for 1 February 1664 refers to 'discourse with the King about an invention of Glasse Granadoes' – the forerunner of the plastic grenade of 1941 – and eighteen months later he 'went to Greenwich where His Majesty was trying divers granados shot of cannon'. A well thrown bomb was invaluable for panicking small parties of Moorish cavalry. With their aid both Charles and Henrietta Forts were held. After some weeks Bridges felt strong enough to begin another fortification, Ann Fort, on a hill quarter of a mile or more in advance of the Catherine Port.

The defeat, however, had dealt a heavy blow to morale. Everybody in the garrison knew that they were able to rout any number of Moors in a stand up fight but being immured in their prison with no prospect of reinforcements sufficient to revenge themselves was too much for the less steady men.

Teviot's ambush had cost almost as many men as Isandhlwana was to do a couple of centuries later, but Isandhlwana was swiftly avenged at Ulundi. No prospect of vengeance appeared for the garrison of Tangier which, as armies do, began to feel itself forgotten when no more troops came. A few deserted by boat to the Spaniards who, if they ran true to form, probably strung them up; some were desperate enough to go over to the Moors and what became of them is not known, though easy to guess. The fact that Teviot had left the Treasury almost empty did not help – Pepys, who was becoming comfortably off from his revenues as Treasurer of Tangier, found his accounts incomprehensible – and something much like a mutiny took place to the cry of 'No money, no guard'. It was undeniable that pay was seven months in arrears but that was something to which Tangier was becoming accustomed. At the critical moment the navy arrived. Two frigates, HMS *Phoenix* and HMS *Advice*, rounded the Mole and dropped anchor as Bridges was debating with himself what to do for the best.

The army pulled itself together and, though Bridges felt obliged to have one mutineer shot, it returned to duty without demur. *Le cafard* seems to have operated long before the Foreign Legion existed. There was one more example to be made. A Mr Wilson, who can hardly have been the same man as the first intelligence officer – Wilsons were fairly thick on the ground in Tangier – was strongly suspected of sending regular reports to the Duke of

Medina Sidonia, who was in turn passing them on to Gayland with even more solid help. He was lucky to suffer nothing worse than imprisonment. Lord Peterborough, to his credit, offered to come back, blaming the whole business firmly on Teviot's rashness. He refused, however, to have any truck with Fitzgerald, the deputy governor now hasting back to his charge. The King refused his well-meant offer.

Fitzgerald arrived in July, to find that Bridges and his officers had matters well in hand again. Fort Ann already stood twenty-six feet high and a new redoubt near the sand-hills, Kendal Fort, was only a little less. One melancholy task had come to Tobias Bridges also. His message to the Countess of Teviot had never caught up with her; the unfortunate lady disembarked at the Mole on 3 June 1664 'full of hope and joy, but now most disconsolate, and she is endeavouring to pay the garrison up to 4 May for my Lord's honour'. The reinforcements that arrived with Fitzgerald brought the strength of the infantry up to about 1,200 and the cavalry to three troops. The foot was again mustered in two regiments, the Governor's and Colonel Norwood's, with strict instructions to avoid any distinction between English, Scotch and Irish. Two more works were put in hand, to protect the workings at Whitby, Henrietta Redoubt and the tiny fortlet at the foot of the cliff which became known as the Devil's Drop[11].' Gayland, who was rumoured to be supplied with Spanish guns and aided by Spanish engineers in Moorish costume, began to build works of his own. The prospect of reducing Fez or anywhere else to King Charles's obedience began to look remote indeed, but the moment of danger to the city had, for the time being, passed.

The remainder of the summer was relatively quiet. Colonel Norwood, who had distinguished himself in every battle in which he was engaged, was sent on a mission to Gayland to negotiate a further peace but came back with an equivocal answer. The King sent five medals and chains to be distributed to those most worthy of them and, as the deputy-governor reported, 'there is much emulation concerning the distributing'. Colonel Alsop and Tobias

Bridges each received one, as they deserved, but no record appears to exist of what happened to the others. The weather was extremely hot and trying: Major Palmes Fairborne, later to be one of the best governors of them all, quarrelled so fiercely with Major White that Bridges felt obliged to place them both under open arrest. When he went to report what he had done Fitzgerald flew into a rage and they came near to blows. A council of war was summoned and peace was made all round, even to the enjoining of Captain Brian 'to ask Lieutenant Harris' pardon for having caned him in the head of the Parade'. Mr Harris does not seem to have been an amiable man. Shortly after this he called out another subaltern named Bassett and killed him. After this bloodletting matters seem to have quietened down. By October Fountain Fort, the well within being one of the most important suppliers of water for the garrison, was finished, 500 palisades were erected around it and the same number around the Devil's Drop. All the senior officers appear to have detested Fitzgerald – the fact that he had been awarded a life pension of £500 for 'good services at Tangier' while those who had done the fighting got nothing may have had something to do with it – but the general situation seemed to be improving. Then, in November 1664, war with Holland became a formal state of affairs and for months afterwards the thunder of the broadsides rumbled down the East Coast from Lowestoft to Deal. Spain, which in September had demanded cession to her of the city of Tangier, was preparing the expedition against Portugal which was to end at Montesclaros. The garrison of Tangier found itself at the end of the queue for everything.

5
Lord Bellasyse

In the Tangier State Papers, its black ink not turned completely to brown, lies a letter from Lord Teviot to Mr Secretary Bennett. It tells of the probable breakdown of negotiations and forthcoming attack by Gayland, which Teviot related with enthusiasm: 'Bon chat, bon rat, we are not made of jelly', and the fight that he and his men made proved the truth of his words. Men of the mettle of Fitzgerald, Alsop, Norwood and Bridges certainly understood what Lord Wellington was to assert so firmly in India later on. Against a primitive enemy – and, despite the memories of past splendours, the Moors of the 1660s were primitive – it is necessary to attack continually and to act with audacity. Now, with the garrison reinforced, the most important of the fortifications finished and the magazines fairly full, was the time to strike Gayland a blow so that he would never again willingly meet a red-coat face to face. It could have been done; with the possession of Tangier assured, the course of the War of the Spanish Succession would have been very different – if, indeed, it would have happened at all. The Dutch, recent victims of Spanish fury and soon to be victims of the ambitions of Louis XIV, made the stroke impossible. With the English fleet fully occupied and convoys carrying men and supplies no longer capable of being counted on, no governor of Tangier would dare risk a punitive expedition which, even if entirely successful, would leave him weakened, possibly to an extent where he could not meet those Moors yet unfought, Ben Barka of Sallee and the Alcaid of Tafiletta, assisted perhaps by a Spanish force from Cadiz or

Ceuta. Gayland was allowed to exult unchecked in his victory, to obtain guns from Spain and to boast, not unreasonably, that he could take Tangier whenever he wanted. Always he had the advantage of the high ground, and always his informants were able to come and go into the city pretty much at will. The garrison could do little beyond keeping up systematic patrolling, pushing on the engineering work of the forts and finding fatigue parties to help the molemen. It is not remarkable that boredom set in.

A faint but perceptible change was coming over Tangier by the beginning of the Dutch war and the year of the Great Plague. The New Model style of soldier was no longer coming with the new drafts and in his place there was drifting in a high proportion of Catholic Irish. The typical soldier was coming closer to a Connaught Ranger of the North-West Frontier in the late nineteenth century than to the zealots who had ridden at Naseby with the 68th Psalm roaring out as they formed line and charged. In appearance also he was beginning to look more like Private Mulvaney than Obadiah-Bind-Their-Kings-In-Chains-And-Their-Nobles-In-Links-Of--Iron. Hollar's portraits at Windsor Castle show sentries in shapeless slouch hats that British soldiers have loved for centuries (the Monmouth cap seems to have been kept for fatigue dress), loose jackets and grey breeches. The painting suggests a texture of cloth thinner than wool and it may easily have been on the walls of Tangier that khaki drill first saw the light of the African day. Most men not on sentry smoked nose-warmer clay pipes, probably loaded with greenish powder which passed for tobacco amongst the Moors. It was better, just, than no tobacco at all. The weapons are still the same; the sentry carries a matchlock, of which presumably the government still had a good many, his sergeant a halberd and the subaltern a sword and a stout stick. The bandolier with its dozen or so charges rattling about in wooden tubes is slung over the right shoulder and under the skirt of the sentinel's coat is his only other personal weapon, a short brass-hilted hanger. There is a professional look about them; Tangier service may not have attracted the cream of the nation's young men but it made real soldiers of those it had. They became hard men, harder than any Civil War troopers and nearer in toughness to men like Pappenheim's Pandours of the Thirty Years War. It was necessary, if they were to survive. Rough the soldiers may have been but they were angels compared to an enemy who regarded cruelty as one of the necessities of life.

Changes had come about also at the top. With so many other and more important troubles nearer home the government could no longer spare well-known and respected men to command an outpost. The truth of the matter was that Tangier needed not so much a general of genius as a competent accountant with experience of fraud work. Too many people, most of them far from the city, were making a comfortable fortune apiece out of the place. The commissioners, including Prince James, Samuel Pepys the Treasurer, various sea captains and their owners and the victualler Mr Yeabsley all had their shares of every payment that could be prised from the Treasury, as did Mr Povey the former Treasurer who had sold his job to Pepys. Some of the toll taken was legitimate or, at least, understandable.

The gradual swing towards a Catholic Ascendancy continued with the next governor. Lord Bellasyse was an Irish soldier of fortune who, had he been born a generation later, would almost certainly have become a Wild Goose. As it was, a Protestant king created him a peer and he embarked for his new command in the *Happy Return* on 22 March 1665. She had come from Tangier and her captain was able to tell Bellasyse with melancholy satisfaction that the pay of the garrison was now ten months in arrears. Bellasyse sailed from Plymouth Sound, the *Happy Return* leading a convoy of the Smyrna fleet escorted by three frigates. With him came a reinforcement of some 200 officers and men, half of them apparently coming from the Plymouth Militia as the Audit Office received a bill for £149 for the cost of their transport.

Lord Bellasyse lacked the social standing of his predecessors but he was a practical man and knew his trade. His first report to the commissioners, dated 12 April 1665, was entirely to the point; if the government reckoned Tangier to be worth keeping it must resign itself to finding £10,000 a year for the fortifications and a further identical sum for keeping up the work of building the Mole. He introduced himself to the hinterland by taking a troop of cavalry to the site of the last disaster, now known as Teviot's Hill. The Moorish cavalry, not having expected this, arrived next day in overwhelming numbers but were too late, 'they not having seen any of ours so far abroad a long time, nor shall not hereafter for our going out is useless and dangerous'.

This was the core of the whole matter. All military sense and instinct demanded that a well-equipped and supplied mounted force be put together and, after intelligence reports had been got and examined, sent to crush Gayland in a pitched battle. The Tangier horse was capable of riding down many times its own number and, suitably reinforced for the occasion, it could probably have hit him such a blow that the city would be thenceforth treated as a hedgehog is by a cat. Those, however, were not the orders Lord Bellasyse received. Not an extra horse-soldier could be sent and he had better confine himself to building forts, enlarging and strengthening the Mole, manning the walls and hoping for better times. All these things Lord Bellasyse obediently did. He should not be blamed for it. Certainly he was not idle. His report to the King despatched in May assures His Majesty of 'a good account of my undertakings, having already in this short time regulated many disorders, dissipated all factions, improved trade, settled the civil authority and encouraged the military.'

The Mole, even in its unfinished state, now showed how valuable an English harbour on the north-west tip of Africa could be. A month after Bellasyse had taken over, the Dutch arrived; a big squadron of eighteen ships of the line or large frigates hovered off Tangier Bay where a number of merchantmen and a few ships of the Royal Navy were at anchor. The Dutchmen hovered about just out of cannon shot but plainly felt disinclined to take on the new ten-gun battery which Bellasyse had set up at the tip of the Mole. When the Levanter blew they sailed away, with no shot having been fired by either side. Their arrival may not have been fortuitous; the Tangier Papers tell of a plot hatched by a Jew, Jacob West, who lived in Tetuan and had agreed with the governor there to persuade Gayland to refuse peace negotiations with Bellasyse, part of the inducement being a blockade of Tangier by forty Dutch frigates. The conjoint effect of a handsome gift from Bellasyse to celebrate his arrival and the evident inability of the Dutch to achieve anything in the face of the English guns swung the Moorish Prince the other way. A polite letter assured Bellasyse that Gayland had wanted only peace with Teviot but that peace had been broken by the governor himself. Had this not happened, peace might have endured as long as Gayland's lived. He was perfectly willing to renew the truce if Lord Bellasyse wished it.

Lord Bellasyse was a Yorkshireman – he had turned out for the King at Marston Moor with the Trained Bands of his county – and, in Yorkshire tradition, he had no passion for foreigners. Gayland, as the governor well knew, had his own tradition, that of the Thames waterman who looks one way and goes another. The handsome gifts he received from the new incumbent, matched only by 'a lean present' returned by him were enough to buy him off for a time but the garrison could not depend on the benevolence of so shifty a neighbour. Gayland was always at pains not to bring about a state of affairs in which diplomatic relations between the city and himself would become broken beyond repair for he had cares of his own and other neighbours who were no more friendly. A small premium, such as allowing Bellasyse to buy fodder and slaughter cattle at a stiff price, would ensure that if he should ever find himself a fugitive there would be a place of refuge at hand where at any rate his life would be safe.

All this was painstakingly explained to the commissioners, accompanied by letters complaining about the meagreness of the supplies now coming in and the precarious condition of a fortress largely dependent on an enemy's goodwill. Bellasyse, however, did not content himself with grumbling and writing letters that would cover him in case of another disaster. Not only did he have to look to his walls and outworks as his predecessors had done but he had also to be ready to fight against any attempt by the powerful Dutch

navy at a sea-landing. The quarrymen of Whitby, never underemployed, were set to work on another battery position on the
Mole, a covered way was laboriously dug out to connect Charles
Fort more securely with the gate at Peterborough Tower and the
civil population were transformed into a militia with defined alarm
posts. The garrison worked with a will, for Bellasyse was no
Restoration fop but a good officer who cared for his men. Under
him, though he could not take credit for it, the soldiers drew their
pay regularly and he was able to assert truthfully that he lost not a
single man during the ever risky duties of getting in forage.

In October 1665 the Admiralty, in spite of all the demands of the
war, was able to scrape together a convoy of twenty 'great and small
ships' to run in supplies. On 22 October anxious watchers on the
tower were able to descry their top-sails, but it was no longer the
proud squadron that had left the Downs. The Dutch had been
waiting in ambush off Cape Spartel and men with perspective
glasses could make out through the clear morning light the clouds
of smoke from the guns, the trailing of shattered masts and spars
and the flames leaping from burning ships. The convoy, by no
means the flower of either Royal or Merchant Navies, was putting
up a poor fight and plainly was getting the worse of the battle,
except in one place. Captain Howard in the little *Merlyn* tore into
the Dutchmen with such determination that they left the attack on
the supply ships to turn on him. *Merlyn*, her guns firing to the last,
was smashed to splinters but most of the convoy was able to escape
and straggle into the bay under the guns of the Mole. Of *Merlyn* no
trace remained but some floating wreckage: she deserves to rank
with *Jervis Bay* and *Rawalpindi*, the first king's ship to sacrifice herself in a battle against impossible odds in order to allow a convoy to
get through. The largest of the victuallers and two merchantmen
fell into Dutch hands but the battered remnant, safe thanks to
Bellasyse's gunners, contained stores enough to keep the garrison
in being for a month or so. Two other victuallers had been sunk,
one ship deserted shamefully to Sallee and the richly-laden argosies
bound for Smyrna had all been lost. The Spaniards were furious at

the relief. Mr Westcombe, the agent at Cadiz, reported to the governor that the Duke of Medina Sidonia told Gayland that he must cut off all communication with Tangier because plague was raging and it was death to enter the place. The agent, better informed, let it be widely known that this was black untruth. 'Tangier is in perfect health', she reported, 'and a great eyesore to the Spaniards'.

Even so, it still had troubles enough. The constantly changing alliances of the second half of the century brought in another enemy with the coming of the year 1666. King Louis joined with the Dutch, made war on England and added another fleet to the potential raiders from the sea. First blood went to Bellasyse even before he knew that war had broken out; a French ship was chased into the bay by a Turkish squadron and was promptly seized. The governor enquired what he should do with her, his only information being that the French had lately pirated a number of English merchantmen. What became of the prize is not clear. It is, however, quite clear that Lord Bellasyse had become disenchanted with the free port of Tangier, a status conferred on it in December 1665. A place at Court was waiting for him – it had probably been kept open on the understanding that he would go and take matters in hand after Teviot's debacle – and he seems to have felt, with some justice, that he had kept his part of the bargain. In January 1666 Bellasyse wrote privately to Arlington, pointing out that he had been very busy with the building of 'new redoubts and breastworks to secure the city against both Dutch and French and expressing the desire to come home' as he conceived his coming would be to the advantage of His Majesty's service. The commissioners raised no objection, but they jibed at the choice of a successor. In Tangier Colonel Fitzgerald seemed the obvious choice. He had long experience of the place and of the people with whom he had to do business and his skill and courage had been amply demonstrated. What looked obvious in Tangier was regarded with dark suspicion in London where the word Papist was enough to damn any man out of hand. There was talk of Tangier being a nest of Popish treason and Fitzgerald, like many of the men in the garrison, was undeniably an Irish Catholic. In the mood of the moment he was unemployable and even his commission as deputy-governor was revoked. In place of both men only one appointment was made; Colonel Henry Norwood was, on 21 February 1666, commissioned lieutenant-governor, 'in the absence of a Governor', a step that served the economic purpose of saving one salary.

Henry Norwood was a good soldier but a fussy man. His letters, dispatches, memoranda and reports, many of them over matters that now seem trivial, exceed by far those of any other governor. He was, for all that, an honest man and generously conceded that when he arrived in the following month he found his new command in a better condition than 'the nature of His Majesty's affairs could promise'. With the fleet laid up and the hour of England's greatest humiliation, the arrival of the Dutch in the Medway, close at hand the nature of His Majesty's affairs could hardly have been regarded as promising. Fortunately neither were those of Gayland.

He had, for some reason, decided to take on the Spanish garrison at Ceuta and had been roundly defeated. When such things happened Gayland usually cast about for friends for he was a great hedger of bets. The new treaty of 2 April 1666 was far more advantageous to Tangier than any previous one, at any rate on paper. It even promised help against any attack by Christians.

The treaty bore the name of Lord Bellasyse, 'Captain-General of all the Forces belonging to His Majesty of Great Britain in Africa, viz. Admiral of his Royal Navy on the Coast of Barbary and Governor of the City of Tangier, etc.', and the notes appended to the copy sent to London did not understate the advantages he had gained. The peace was to be perpetual, no mere six months armistice, 'we are to have all provisions out of his country, woods etc.' and 'we are to have no guards imposed on us by Gayland (over foraging parties) what was a great encumbrance to the garrison and for which my Lord Teviot paid £500 per annum'; moreover 'we have stones for carrying on the Mole; we pay the same quantity of powder annually as my Lord Teviot did and have ground granted without our lines of double value'. The bargain was no less good for 'The Most Excellent Cidi Hamet Hader Ben Ali Gayland, Prince of West Barbary, Arzilla,

Alcassar, Tituan, Saly, etc.', and it answered his immediate purpose. When a French fleet hove in sight a few days later he was as apprehensive of an attack on Sallee as Norwood was anxious to receive one on Tangier. Metaphorically rolling up his sleeves the governor informed Whitehall that he was 'in so good a condition for their reception and welcome at Tangier as shall tell the world how vainly they have sought and found their ruin'. The French admiral took the same view; the batteries on the Mole and the great parade ground by the beach from which it protruded looked altogether too businesslike for him to take them on and he set course instead for the roadstead of Cadiz. Norwood, like the sensible man he was, turned his attention to the landward defences; the treaty had expressly forbidden the making of any new works but did not inhibit the completion of those existing or at least begun. Catherine Port was strengthened with 'palisadoes and turn-pikes' and the protection of Whitby was secured by strengthening the small blockhouse called the Devil's Drop; the Mole was far from complete and the safety of the men working on it was always a first charge on the resources.

Gayland did not have to wait long for the return of the bread he had cast on the waters. His rough handling by the Spaniards was the signal for which his enemies had been waiting, an indication that his power was declining. His old rival the Emir of Taffiletta moved in for the kill and Gayland's soldiers deserted by companies. A judicious outlay of presents bought most of the governors of Gayland's cities and by the end of June 1666 he was immured in his last stronghold of Arzilla, wounded in five places and abandoned by all but a handful of his followers. Now was the time to call upon the Kafirs, the unbelievers, since only they could save him from a protracted death. From Arzilla a trusted courier rode out on the last day of the month and made his way safely to the Catherine Port. 'Excellent Sir', ran his message,

> All places are overspread with disasters and events of our war. The ill success of this time befallen me hath been by the design of my enemy… who, falling in with his army,

surprised my careless out-guards and broke and rooted (sic) the whole body. Upon notice whereof I got on horseback at Alcazar but found my people running away in so great disorder that it exceeded my power to rally them till I came to Arzilm. Whence I am now necessitated to crave your Excellencie's assistance upon the account of that Peace and Friendship solemnly contracted between us and therefore desire that you would send me a boat of good bigness that if I should be put to any straight I might send to you for succour, which I doubt not but your Excellency will please to send me upon honourable terms.

Norwood, though uneasy at the prospect of having to face a new and stronger enemy as the price of keeping his word, promptly did all that was asked of him, including the dispatch of a surgeon to dress Gayland's wounds. The knowledge that he had a safe place of refuge put new heart into the Moorish chieftain who, whatever his faults, was a man of valour. As he recovered from his hurts he managed to keep his walls manned and, as more and more of his kinsfolk came to join him, he managed an occasional raid upon the besieger's lines. It was, however, plain that he could not hold out forever and a worried Colonel Norwood had to plan to receive an attack on his landward defences in greater strength than anything that had gone before. He did not allow the possibility to weaken his resolve. As he wrote to Arlington in July, the garrison was 'both able and willing to withstand Taffileta'. There was no softening of the military qualities of the Tangier Regiment during the balmy nights of summer; the first soldiers of the regular army set those who came after as good an example as any could wish. The molemen also went their sturdy way; by July their work jutted out into deep water 200 yards from the shore. The merchants of the town put it to good use by fitting out five ships as privateers and picking up welcome prizes which they towed back to sanctuary.

It was not only booty that the prizes furnished but also another commodity which the garrison needed even more. Like so many

Britons in the generations to follow, expatriate and seemingly for-gotten, they wanted above all things news of home and the garbled reports that filtered through Spain were demonstrably unreliable, Spain and the United Provinces seemed to have sunk their differ-ences. The Manila and Acapulco galleons still made their regular passages but the Spanish fleets were now a gilded phantom of van-ished glories; the Dutch, whose great empires of the East and the West had turned them into the merchants of the world, had strong commercial instincts. Much of the best blood of Holland had been spilled by the Spaniard and there was a long account to settle. From a practical point of view Spanish gold was a more marketable com-modity than Spanish blood and, by degrees; the ships of Amsterdam and Zeeland were becoming the carriers not only for their own Ceylon and East Indies but also for Spanish America. As King Louis had decided the genius of France should reside in the barrack-room rather than the forecastle, the navies of France, for the moment, were not at their full strength. Hispano-Dutch shipping lanes girdled the earth, so far as it was then known, and Tangier might easily have become the lion in their path. A combination of factors irrelevant to strategy, mostly of a religious and a financial kind, inhibited this hap-pening. As a result of the internal strife in England the navy – a navy containing men of the quality of Christopher Myngs and John Narborough and which John Evelyn called 'the most glorious fleet that ever set sails' – was laid up in ordinary and, even after their defeat at the great battle off Lowestoft, the Dutch were given a walk-over. Tangier had ceased to be a gap through which the England of King Charles might spread its civilising and colonizing mission through-out Morocco. No new places would be reduced to His Majesty's obedience and Tangier must look after itself as best it could without any particular ambition save as a useful haven in times of trouble.

It was the loot from privateering that paid the bills during the hardest times. Colonel Norwood (who seems to have had another source of income since he is described in all official documents as 'Treasurer of the Colony of Virginia' as well as lieutenant-governor of Tangier) said so flatly. 'Our privateering hath very much conduced to the enriching of this place if not to its preservation' runs one of his regular dispatches dated 20 March 1666 in which he tells of selling prizes and seizing about 4,500 bushels of wheat. Some of the captures were lawful acts of private war but, to shipmasters other than English, the corsairs of Tangier differed only from those of Sallee in that they did not make slaves of their prisoners. Retaliation naturally followed and there seems a rather unreasonable querulousness over Norwood's complaint in February 1667 that the Spaniards had snatched up a pink found becalmed off Cadiz. These were not his only troubles. During the same month a great storm did more than £1,000 worth of damage to the houses and lack of timber made their repair a slow business.

A combination of heat, short commons and Irish temper occasionally troubled the good discipline which the lieutenant-governor kept. The most notable of a number of duels again involved Palmes Fairborne and it has very much the look of a forced quarrel. One of the many Fitzgeralds at Tangier was a subaltern and an insubordinate one.

On an evening in February 1667 he enquired of Major Fairborne whether it was his night for guard. When Fairborne told him that it was he grumbled that he had made an exchange with another officer. Fairborne, very properly, told him that his name was top of the roster whereupon Fitzgerald flew into a rage, announcing that he knew his duty as well as any man in the town. Fairborne, who was carrying a stick, seems to have made some gesture with it and Fitzgerald half drew his sword, crying out 'You do not intend to cane me?' Fairborne, in the presence of 'Master Robert the Apothecary', and a Mr White, said that he had no intention of doing anything of the kind but ordered Fitzgerald into close arrest for insolence. Within minutes a Lieutenant-Colonel Fitzgerald, described in the reports as a 'kinsman', arrived on the scene, blustered loudly and called Fairborne out. Fairborne, having no choice, accompanied the Irishman to a convenient place.

Whatever Norwood might have felt like doing he could not afford to deprive his garrison of two experienced field officers. He spoke soothing words, ordered young Fitzgerald to apologise and satisfied honour all round. His private opinion was put in a letter to Mr Williamson, Lord Arlington's secretary and a close friend of Fairborne: it would be for the good of the garrison if the house of Fitzgerald could be employed somewhere else.[12] The State Papers are silent as to whether he had his way. Norwood, having given up any idea of becoming governor himself, wrote to Lord Bellasyse on 3 March 1667. 'I wish His Majesty may fix on someone who will engage to settle here for life'. His hope was vain, for Tangier had a lack of attraction sufficient to induce any great man to want to end his days there. The petition of Colonel William Johnson shows some of the reasons. After reminding the commissioners that he had served for twenty-eight years under two kings, the colonel, who was Judge of the Admiralty Court, came to the nub of the matter. He had had no pay for two years, 'money for prizes taken or sold being paid to the Lord Ashley Cooper'. Fairborne, in one of his letters to Williamson, wrote of his own views on the subject. He complained of the frequent changes and added gloomily that he himself could expect no advancement because 'every Governor-General brings his own creatures with him'.

One aspirant was not put off by these venalities. Sir Hugh Cholmley, the Mole expert, saw himself as the stuff of which governors are made and announced his willingness to accept the office, pointing out how his previous services and financial losses gave him a strong claim. The commissioners took a different view and declined to press the King to appoint him. With Taffiletta's army not far away, with a garrison now down to 1,200 effective men of whom about a quarter were employed about the Mole and a worrisome shortage of new guns and ammunition it was a different kind of talent that Tangier would be needing. In fact the strength of the force was not reduced quite so low – allowance must be made for temporary sick – for the establishment of January 1668 puts it at one regiment of 1,400 men and half a troop of horse. On paper they were well paid. A Captain, for example, was entitled to 8s a day, which does not compare badly with the 17s 6d he drew in 1939: a private soldier at a daily rate of 9d would have been quite rich. It was of little more than academic interest as they were seldom paid at all.

The new establishment put the cost of maintaining Tangier at a few shillings under £8,000 a quarter for pay alone and a number of men were sent home for reasons of economy. It is fair to assume that most of these were the least valuable but there was one man who could not easily be replaced. 'Ned Witham, whose valour and discretion hath been ever highly extolled amongst us', as Fairborne wrote to Williamson, had never been more than captain but had acted as staff officer to the lieutenant-governor, as his signature to many official letters testifies. It was probably Witham who spoke to Prince Rupert at Whitehall on 15 May 1668 where the twenty-three gentlemen who made up the Tangier Commission were assembled to discuss the city's affairs. The weakness of the place must have been strongly represented by some person who spoke with authority and persuasiveness for the order went out that the 400 troops still in Portugal should go to Tangier, half to increase the garrison's strength and half to replace men lately returned home.

It was just about in time for in July Gayland, his men having turned against him, arrived by sea with 360 followers, now his entire array. It was not until after Colonel Norwood had given him sanctuary that the Moor disclosed that he had also brought the contents of his treasury amounting to some three million pieces of eight. It was probably the first instance of Arab money sustaining British arms. Norwood, as he wrote to the Lieutenant of the Ordnance, Colonel William Legge, had received none from home since the previous November and could only exist by borrowing. The takings from privateering activities seem to have fallen off.

No money came but instead Tangier was created a borough, with a mayor, a recorder, six aldermen and a dozen councillors, to be drawn from the few hundred inhabitants and to relieve the governor of some of his more tiresome civil functions. The first mayor, a Mr Bland, was well aware of the dignities of his ancient office. Fairborne, who watched his pretensions with quiet amusement, wrote to Williamson that 'was not the soldierly part well governed and the officers a good tempered set of gentlemen, Mr Bland's great pride, with his foolishness, would soon breed a great distraction amongst us'. A beleaguered garrison is not the ideal locality for displays of civic pomp.

The garrison was, by the early part of 1669, in its weakest state since the city had passed to the crown of England and the council of Tangier was well aware of the fact. The setting-up of a civil administration, complete with its Court of Justice and Bench of Aldermen, had been intended to relieve the soldiers of some duties but the remedy was as efficacious as providing a wheel-chair for a man bleeding to death. The King, though always well disposed to his wife's estate, had troubles enough of his own; the springtime of the Restoration was now only a memory, the brief summer had flowered and gone and autumn was setting in. The moment of the city's greatest need yet coincided with his own most desperate financial straits and already his thoughts were turning towards calling upon his cousin Louis for the funds needed to keep the monarchy afloat. The decision that was to lead in the following year to the secret Treaty of Dover was not an easy one for the King, quite apart from the considerations of religion that plagued the latter part of the seventeenth century. Although both Charles and Louis were the grand-children of Henry of Navarre (from whom both inherited a refined appetite for beautiful women) and personally not antagonistic to each other their interests were by no means identical. Each King had a stake in the North American continent, that of France being the greater, and the nightmare that never quite left the English monarch was that of a Franco-Dutch partnership taking over all trade with these lands of the future. Holland already had become a world power with holdings not only in the New World but even further afield. Suzerainty of the East Indies had already passed from Portugal, the Cape of Good Hope was in Dutch hands and Dutch forts were scattered along the west coast of Africa where they were acquiring an air of permanence. Louis had his own plans for the future of metropolitan Holland, plans that would keep wars going in Europe until well into the next century and for the moment it was to England's interest to put such money as it had on the French horse. It had no choice.

War between the opposing Moorish factions, never entirely quiescent, had flared up again and once more Gayland was getting the worst of it. In May, just as the council was meeting, his troops mutinied and once again he made for the sanctuary of Tangier. No serious attack followed, much to the garrison's relief, and on 23 September a reinforcement of 400 trained soldiers, the remnant of the force that had been in Portugal, disembarked. Norwood was well pleased with their looks, 'very brave men' he called them, and it gave him the opportunity to rid himself of 130 of his useless mouths. It was, however, less comforting for him to contemplate the condition of his command, for Tangier had sunk to a very low ebb. Food was shorter than the oldest hand could remember; pay was already a full year behind hand and the state of both the walls and the forts was deplorable. Stores of every kind were close to exhaustion and, as the lieutenant-governor wrote in his report, 'the burden on him was almost unsupportable'.

Fairborne, never a man to exaggerate his hardships, told his friend Mr Williamson that 'Tangier was never in worse condition than at present. I hope some care is taken to remedy this or else the Lord have mercy upon us'.

The Moors, under the victorious Taffiletta, moved in closer, becoming daily more active and menacing. No record has come down of the innumerable small fights between the garrisons of the outlying posts and the parties that lay in ambush to catch them as every guard was changed but they appear to have been almost daily affairs. The troops, about 1,500 strong now and organised as a single regiment with half a troop of horse, behaved throughout with a bravery and resolution that compel respect.

The Tangier garrison, lumped together over its twenty years or so of existence, has come down through history with a bad name, entirely owing to the fact that Whig historians – Thomas Babington Macaulay at their head – seized on the bad conduct of a few men after Sedgmoor as being typical of the brutalizing effect of service in this forgotten outpost. The truth is other than that. Only thoroughly disciplined men, led by officers whom they trusted, could have endured their privations and come up time and again with their weapons clean, with the heart to take on an enemy as savage and treacherous as any Afridi or Pathan and to get the better of them every time, without even the advantage of superior armament. It was inevitable that once in a while a man would succumb and make a desperate bid to desert. Fairborne put a stop to one such endeavour on the day following Christmas 1669.

As affairs were calmer he decided to ride about the lines with his wife. When they approached James Fort there was a burst of firing and Fairborne was told that a man had run away to the enemy and was already out of range. Coolly handing his wife over to the fort commander Fairborne rode after the deserter, heading straight towards a substantial body of Moors, caught up with him and brought him back at pistol point; he then took up his wife again and finished his tour of inspection. The man was court-martialled and hanged a few days later. Such was the quality of the officers who held the neglected citadel for their King throughout the long years of thankless and unrewarded privation. Pride of race, pride of regiment and the willing assumption of duty made them what they were and there, in Tangier, the concept of duty that we know today was born.

The King, it is fair to assume, did his limited best for this outlying parcel of his realm but one cannot avoid feeling that he might have done better. Mr Lloyd George once remarked that a fully equipped duke cost more to maintain than a fully equipped battleship: a fully equipped mistress probably cost at least as much as three months rations for a regiment and half a troop of horse. Though the idea of the conquest of Morocco had long been given up, the conquests of Louise de Kerouaille and the Mazarine were less arduous and more immediately rewarding even though there might have been little to choose between their respective costs. The revenue never exceeded one and a half million pounds a year and Tangier accounted for a disproportionate part of it. Even so, it did disgorge £10,000 at the end of 1669 which, according to Norwood, 'cheered our hearts'. It did little beyond that.

Colonel Norwood's heart stood in need of cheer. He explained the reason in a letter to his friend Colonel Legge on 10 November.

> I am gotten out of the frying pan into the fire; no sooner escaped the fury of the Turks but I sum by the ears with a Mayor of Tangiers. I know I must be tender of Corporations; they have been much blessed birds unto the Crown... I thought within this month that Satan himself in person could not have put me into any manner of disorder with this man, nor could I have been brought to be in earnest with him unless his malice had been such as you will see of much ill consequence to the garrison.

Mr Bland, who would have remembered the rule of Cromwell's major-generals, was plainly a man determined to assert the superiority of the civil over the military power so long as it was safe to do so. Many years were to pass before a sensible *modus vivendi* between the two would exist in the settlements overseas that became an empire.

There was another worry almost as serious as the weakness of the army's hold on this pimple on the face of Africa. Without the Mole Tangier was nothing, and the Mole was breaking up. Sir Hugh Cholmley, last survivor of the original commissioners, wrote a report which may well have been modified from strict truth in order to cover up his own deficiencies.

> The Mole had now for about three years advanced with continual good progress and approbation, the carts bringing daily great quantities of stone without any obstruction from the storms and the weather, and the work not having received from the sea the least of damage; but about the end of December in this year and the beginning of January fol-

lowing happened the first breach, the noise of which filled all the gazettes of Europe; and though this was in consequence no more than what is usual in such like works, it was, however, represented in England with so much inflammation, on the one hand, and again on the other so much lessened, that the truth of the bare matter according to fact was hard to be judged by those that were unbiased in the affair.

Fairborne, who was certainly unbiased, had no faith in the structure as it stood. 'I do believe that it can never be effective unless they build in chests, as they have at Leghorn and Genoa'. The moment for taking it in hand was not now, for the Moors were creeping ever closer. On 2 February 1669 Norwood wrote to Lord Arlington that 'they are plowing ground nearer to the fort this year than ever' and it was rumoured that they had acquired a train of artillery. This, if true, would be serious indeed and gave cause to wonder whether the entire city might not become impossible to hold.

6
Lord Middleton

The attack began in June 1669. Early in the month bands of Moors, both horse and foot, appeared in great numbers and made no secret of prospecting the defences. On 27 June the alert sentries at Cambridge Fort spotted that something was going on in the half-light of dawn and soon it became plain that a considerable ambush had been laid to catch the relieving guard which would arrive early in the afternoon. The guns of the fort, aided by enfilade fire from Fort Bellasyse and the battery on the walls above the Catherine Port, blazed out and the enemy scattered leaving a number of dead behind them. Four days later they attempted another ambush, this time in Ann Lane, the covered way leading from Catherine Port to Fort Ann. Once again the ambushers were dispersed by cannon fire, though every salvo meant a diminution of the tiny stock of powder and shot that seemed unlikely ever to be replaced. Then, early in the morning of 2 July, Tafiletta shifted his ground towards Whitby and the Western Cove in an attempt to waylay the reliefs to Charles and Henrietta Forts and the small blockhouse of the Devil's Drop on the beach. Norwood, wise by now in the ways of his enemy, gave them no chance. The Forts were armed and victualled for a fortnight and he had made arrangements not to be caught by surprise.

> The enemy being discovered by the barking of dogs which are purposely kept thereby, our people and sol-diers with so much readiness appeared with their arms and grenadoes to oppose them, which they taking notice

of immediately withdrew, but not without many shot,
and some men killed, whom they were seen to drag away
between the palisadoes and the sea,

ran the laconic report in the *London Gazette* of 24 July. Undeterred,
the Moors again switched their attack to the south-east face again
and at 9 p.m. that night masses of them appeared between James and
Monmouth Forts evidently bent on rushing Catherine Port.
Colonel Norwood had no intention of merely standing on his walls
and shooting down. Major Fairborne, always in the forefront of the
battle, was ordered out with 150 men under two subalterns named
Philpot and Fitzgerald (probably Fairborne's old antagonist, but a
good fighting man none the less) to see them off. Fairborne determined to teach the Moors a lesson that they would be in no hurry to
forget, took his company between the two forts in order to have his
flanks covered by fire and tore into the tribesmen with pike, musket
and grenade. It is impossible even to guess at the numbers of the
enemy; the report in the Tangier State Papers puts it, 'after a hot dispute for an hour the enemy was forced to retire with considerable
loss, and we consider some great man slain by hearing three salvoes
of shot fired by the enemy, we think for the funeral'. The terse prose
gives little idea of the ferocity of that hour of hand-to-hand fighting.
In the matter of weapons the two sides were evenly matched and the
Moor has always been as brave a man as ever drew breath. For a company of foot to have held together and driven away many times their
number of skilful and bloodthirsty warriors, the fight swaying to and
fro for a long hour, was a feat of arms as fine as anything that a single
unit of the army has ever done. Sixteen days later Fairborne and his
men did it again, on the same ground, when a body of Moorish foot

drew to the sandhills between James and Monmouth
Forts, whereon the lieutenant-governor commanded
Major Fairborne with a good party of musketeers to the
line, where began a warm dispute for over an hour after,
whereon the enemy with considerable loss retired; the

Garrison receiving no hurt but only the death of one corporal.

The army of Charles, overshadowed by that of Queen Anne, has never received much recognition but the flat language of the *Gazette* cannot wholly conceal the skill at arms, the hard discipline and the fierce determination of officers and men who could overcome such odds at so little cost to themselves. There is no harm in the reminder that Britain produced good soldiers between Cromwell and Marlborough. Oliver would, indeed, have been proud of his successors. The young John Churchill, who would then have been twenty years old, is believed to have served as an ensign at Tangier at about this time. It is not impossible that he learnt the elements of his trade under Palmes Fairborne and some of the lessons of that remarkable man would have been at least as useful to a regimental officer as anything he might have picked up under the tutelage of Turenne. With Fairborne's two successes to think about, the Moors abandoned for the present their attempt to storm the city; although this meant that the city was not yet in any danger of being taken by storm, the situation of the garrison was far from being a happy one. Sickness was running at a rate too high for comfort, with men being admitted to hospital at the rate of about ten a day and the cost of their maintenance was heavy.

According to the Audit Office Accounts no less a sum than £2,019 had had to be found over the previous three years merely to keep the sick alive, and there seemed no prospect of the burden ever becoming lighter. One more effort at diplomacy seemed worth making and in September 1669 Lord Henry Howard arrived with an embassy charged with reaching some accommodation with Taffiletta, the man who seemed to hold all the Moorish power in the neighbourhood.

The exercise was futile. Howard came with 'a great train' but failed to make any contact with the effective ruler. After two months, during which 'sports were got up to relieve the dullness of the place by day, such as backsword, wrestling, ball and cudgel play and bull-baiting, and at night twice a week the recreation of dancing', he accepted defeat and went home. Before he left, however, he was able to welcome a new governor, much to the relief of Colonel Norwood who was at last able to devote his energies to the affairs of Virginia. On 9 October 1669 a salute of guns from the Bay announced the arrival of Lord Middleton.

Middleton, a Scot, had the qualities that a Colonial governor has always needed. His brief from the council included no instructions about bringing further expanses of Africa into the King's obedience; such an idea had long ago been tacitly abandoned. His main purpose was to maintain Tangier as a trading station, much as the Dutch were maintaining the Cape of Good Hope, and, if at all possible, to make the place support itself. He needed no telling that it was going to be an uphill struggle.

Mr Bland had returned from a short self-imposed exile in Spain and was swift to thrust under the governor's nose his claims to civic precedence. Middleton managed the difficult feat of humouring the mayor whilst avoiding any falling out with the military authorities. He brought with him the King's order to dub Fairborne a knight, a well-merited honour that pleased the soldiers. The civil population was equally well pleased by his setting up of markets free to all comers, a measure that promptly halved the prices of provisions. As everybody's pay was now about fifteen months in arrears the move was understandably popular, except amongst the holders of market franchises, but it did nothing to furnish more corn, more beef or any other necessary commodity. For the moment, however, the spirits of all the inhabitants rose appreciably.

Sir Hugh Cholmley was delighted. 'In a little time there was a public harmony and peace', he wrote, and from his own point of view the new governor was just the man he sought; Lord Middleton well understood the importance of the Great Mole. It did not take him long to realize that the damage caused by the storms was very serious indeed and, at his urgent request, Cholmley came back in April 1670 to put it to rights. The Tangier Plans in the Royal Library at Windsor Castle specify what needed to be done.

The design of a new quay or causeway from the town to the Mole, a hundred yards whereof being almost finished and a greater part of the foundation stones of the rest already laid. The security of the works on this side of the town which are ruinous and all ready to fall. The great furtherance of His Majesty's service by a nearer and easier communication between the City and the Mole, together with the encouragement of commerce to which this work much conducts were the principal considerations inducing to these useful designs.

Middleton did his best to translate plans into works. From beginning to end the Mole absorbed 167,000 tons of stone (some from the Aislaby quarry near Whitby). One of his first letters as governor, after making the usual complaints about 'the great scarcity of provisions', urges the need of more molemen as well as another 400 foot and eighty horse; he suggested, sensibly enough, that these be raised in Scotland, 'to avoid the expense to England'. It is not impossible that the large proportion of Catholic Irish in the garrison gave him cause to desire a counter-weight. Be that as it may, no more troops came. The best the council could do in the months before the secret Treaty of Dover was to give the serving officers written assurance that promotion should henceforth be made by merit within the existing establishment and that 'no new man be appointed to the supplanting of others in the garrison'.

Unpaid, often hungry, under-equipped and with little prospect of any relief, the soldiers maintained their discipline and fighting spirit in a wonderful manner. The pressure of the Moors never let up.

By the time Sir Hugh returned to Tangier a considerable political change had taken place in the Empire of Morocco. Both Taffiletta and Gayland were dead. The former had died of injuries from a riding accident on 27 March 1672; the latter, who had quitted the discomforts of Tangier for the comparative luxury of Algiers, had lost no time in asserting his claim to the throne of Fez, now occupied by Taffiletta's nephew Muley Ismail. The situation was not hopeless, although he was obliged to begin with very narrow resources, since the straits to which the garrison had been reduced were to him an advantage. On the whole Gayland had honoured his commitments and, in any event, he was the devil Lord Middleton knew. Better to see him as the ruler of Morocco than a stranger of whom little was known beyond a reputation for savage cruelty of a quality noted even by the Moors. So low had the fortunes of Tangier sunk by 1672 that Middleton was compelled to the shameful expedient of selling whatever weapons he could spare in order to buy the means of remaining alive. As Middleton explained in a letter to the King on 3 March 1672, 'peace with the Moor had been the preservation of the place, he wanting arms and they food'. With English guns and ammunition at his disposal, Gayland had no difficulty in winning back to his allegiance some of his old chieftains and soon he was at the head of an respectable army. Muley Ismail, having already overcome his brother Muley Achmet, marched north from Fez to meet his challenger. A battle took place near Alcazar which ended with the head of Gayland impaled on a lance being trooped through the Emperor's camp. From all accounts the old Moor had fought like a hero, four horses being killed under him before a musket ball tumbled him from the saddle.

The news of the death of their old enemy brought no comfort to Lord Middleton. The treaties had been purely personal affairs, in no way binding upon Gayland's successors, and the garrison was in a worse plight than ever before. The State Papers set out the depth to which it had sunk. For a garrison of 1,540 men and some hundreds of civilians there existed, on 4 June 1672, biscuit for three weeks, beef for sixteen, peas and oatmeal none, butter for two weeks and no cheese. Pay was now twenty-six months behind hand. There was open war with the great sea power of Holland and rumours of impending war with Holland's friend Spain.

Nor was there any reason to expect better things in the foreseeable future. By a series of shifts and expedients of which no record has come down, Middleton contrived to keep his people alive and

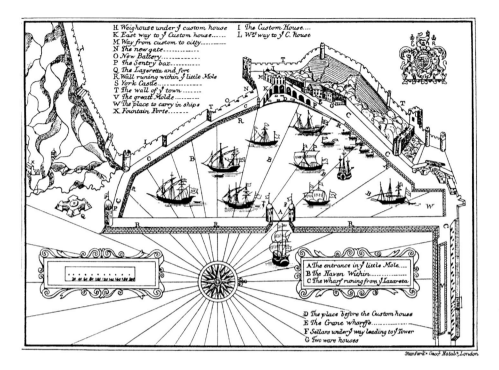

3. The little Mole, showing the wharf and Custom House, 1675.

in tolerably good heart. Privateering no doubt supplied some of their wants for, with both Dutch and Spanish ships having become lawful plunder, it was the only way of filling empty bellies and keeping some store of powder and shot in magazines that were crumbling for want of repair. Fortunately for the garrison the new Emperor was too much occupied with the problems of a disputed succession to have much time for bothering about Tangier.

The years 1673 and 1674 passed without much in the way of military activity. By the winter, however, it had become plain that something must be done about the Mole. Sir Hugh Cholmley had once more returned home, unable to do more than running repairs, and the winter of 1674 was a hard one. Before leaving Sir Hugh had set his men to work sealing up the head of the bay with the little Mole, creating a wet-dock where ships could be careened. Nothing more was possible.

Shere was still pressing for his chest system to be adopted, though Sir Hugh went only part of the way with him. The difference between them was that Shere envisaged the use of great masses of masonry bonded into one piece whereas Cholmley reckoned this beyond the powers of his molemen. His preference was indeed for chests but for more and smaller ones. Each attempted to undercut the other on prices. In the end Shere had his tender accepted, with the proviso that he should have a reward of £2,000 if he succeeded but nothing at all in the event of failure. Very bravely he took the bet and sailed for the Straits early in 1675. Whilst he was still at sea news came that Lord Middleton had died at his post, worn out by privation and worry.

His successor, the Irish Lord Inchiquin, arrived in March. At about the same time an embassy was sent by the King to bargain with the new emperor for something like a permanent peace. It had little more success than that of Lord Henry Howard. Muley Ismail appeared willing enough to enter into some sort of convention but he was promptly over-ruled by one of his holy men who asserted that the Prophet had, on the previous night, appeared to him in a vision, and announced that the Emperor would vanquish all his foes so long as he made no peace with the English. Against his ecclesiastics no emperor can prevail. The embassy was courteously dismissed and the holy man put to the test.

An ambush bigger than the usual ones was planted between some of the outlying forts. For once the defenders seem to have bungled their work; Inchiquin explained that 'the forlorn was allowed to advance too far without support from the main body under Sir Palmes Fairborne and also for allowing Captain Boynton's party to be withdrawn from Ann Lane'.

No great harm came of it, however, for the guards in the forts were as alert as ever and broke up the assault by cannon fire. Only one man was killed and Muley Ismail may have wondered how reliable his seer could have been. A subsequent attempt on the molemen around Whitby was equally roughly handled; the chief Boulif was killed and the governor of Alcazar had a hand shot off.

The garrison received some small additional cheer: during the month of March six months pay arrived, reducing the arrears to a mere two years. The governor went home on leave in April leaving his office to be held jointly by Colonels Alsop and Fairborne. As Alsop was in poor health he relinquished his share in the command and Fairborne was able to take matters properly in hand.

For the first time since Norwood's day every company and every part of the militia was given its proper alarm post. Guard mounting time was altered from mid-afternoon to 7 a.m. so as to deprive men of the opportunity to arrive on parade the worse for drink – 'a shame to the parade and a reproach to the spectators', as the acting-governor reasonably called it. His six months pay soon went in raising the height of some of the outside earthworks where men were constantly being sniped and in having a palisade erected in front of the Main Guard. From the magazines he had a number of dismounted guns dragged out, fitted twenty-four of them with makeshift carriages and filled in the gaps in the walls. The ways to James and Ann Forts – regular sites for ambushes – were banked up to a height of four feet and the line between James and Monmouth Forts finished off. It says much for the relief that soldiers felt at the strong hand of a professional at work that they carried out all these last works at no cost 'except a little brandy to encourage the men'. Having no axe of his own to grind at home he wrote official letters of a strength to which the commissioners were not accustomed. The establishment, still only of one regiment, was 324 men short. As a result 'the soldier is at the third night's duty and three hours sentry and sometimes are forced to do double duty'. He did not exaggerate the disgraceful treatment to which his men were being subjected. In May 1676 came the first mutiny, of which he received warning from an Egyptian servant. Fairborne had ordered a large fatigue party to parade in the market square at 5 p.m. As he arrived to take command a concerted shout went up, 'Home, home'. Fairborne commanded silence and was obeyed. When he asked for an explanation he was told that it was for want of pay – about 2 1/4 years late – and rations, some men grumbling also about the recent extra work.

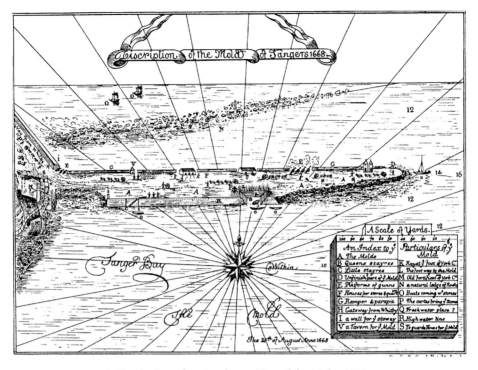

4. Tangier Bay, showing the position of the Mole, 1668.

Fairborne swore that it was all for the King's service and 'for which I would hazard ten thousand lives if I had them', adding that the work had had to be stopped anyway for want of money. He was a just and a kindly governor but mutiny is the one crime that cannot be passed over, more especially where there are no other troops in call but other mutineers or potential mutineers. A court martial on the ring-leaders was promptly convened; after proper trial five were sentenced to death by firing squad, five to the more shameful death by hanging and various lesser offenders were sent to ride the wooden horse. By the time the trial was over most men understood the enormity of what they had done and Fairborne felt able to relent a little. Two only were shot and the remainder freed against promises of future good behaviour. All had the honesty to say that they would do their duty faithfully so long as they were paid and fed but that 'they could not remain passive if they were kept without

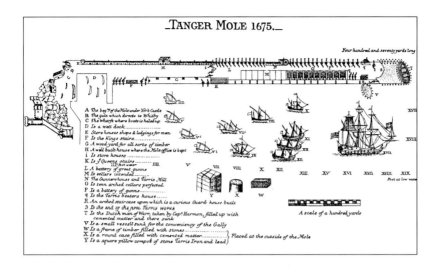

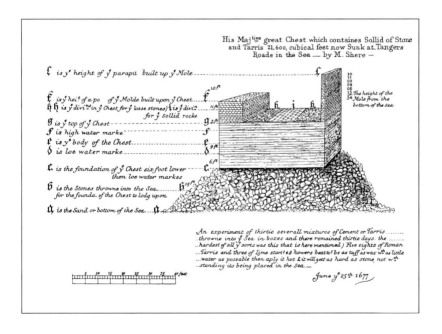

5. Plan of the Mole at Tangier in 1675.

6. The Great Chest constructed for the Mole by Mr Shere, 1677.

both'. It was the best that Fairborne could have expected and it seems probable that only the strength of his personality and the affection soldiers feel for a brave and competent leader that prevented something much worse.

July 1675 gave the acting-governor a chance to try his hand as a diplomat. The famous Admiral Sir John Narborough arrived with a squadron off Tangier and Fairborne thought to seize the chance to give Muley Ismail, then at Sallee, a sight of the Royal Navy and a suggestion that peace with the master of such a power was desirable. Sir John declined to go in person – he had much else to do – but the opportunity was taken of letting Mayor Bland put on a demonstration of civic pomp. He seems to have managed it extremely well, for the mayor and Captain Leslie came back a month later with a treaty of peace between His Majesty King Charles and 'Abunazar Muley Ismail, Emperor of the Kingdoms of Fez, Morocco, Taffiletta, Sus, and of all Algeria and its towns'. Shortly afterwards old Colonel Alsop died, leaving Sir Palmes Fairborne alone as the King's vice-gerent.

7
The Great Mole

Without the Mole Tangier could be nothing more than a luxury that the King could not afford, and the state of the Mole, ten years and more after its beginning, was deplorable. Nobody could be blamed for it; the lessons of similar works in the great inland sea were sound enough in principle but the Atlantic is not the Mediterranean. Tides and storms, breakers and surf all tore at the structure and no man living was in any case to point to a comparable one with comparable difficulties. Not Imperial Rome itself had ever built anything like this but built it had to be or Tangier would wither on the vine. Henry Shere had the heart of the matter but even he had to learn as he went along.

The report that Inchiquin had despatched to the King in March of 1676 gave little encouragement.

> To the eastward of the great chest five chests sunk this year are shattered, but the greatest part of them yet remain. The chest at the end remains entire with the two other small chests placed to the southward for securing the end with the tarras work upon them. The three tally chests sunk before the storms remain firm and entire. The Breakwater is much enlarged.

The worst damage had been suffered by the eastern side where a great breach had appeared and all the facings had collapsed into the sea. On the whole the chest system seemed to have worked but all experience now showed that more and even bigger chests were going to be needed in order to produce the solid wall that was so essential. Plan after plan found its way to Whitehall, with Shere, Cholmley, Fairborne and a number of enthusiastic amateurs all having suggestions to make. Nobody seems to have taken more than a passing interest in any but Shere's last plan, delivered in the following November and the molemen continued their heavy and slow labours under his direction. Each chest was given a name. York, Peterborough, Anglesey, Coventry and Craven led out seawards and at the very end was to be sunk the greatest of them all, the chest called Charles. Reports of progress were irregular and it is not possible to say with any certainty how far the task had advanced at any given time. It is, however, shown in one of the plans submitted by Fairborne that during the year 1676 only York chest had been fabricated and got into place. He describes it as having been placed 'at the bend and most exposed part of the work, manifestly preserving the length of the Mole' and it seems to have met with the success that its designer merited. No details have come down as to the method used of moving it; the most probable seems to be that it was floated into position on some sort of a lighter which was then scuttled. Whatever the method used it was a very considerable feat of engineering. To build a solid edifice 450 yards long and of a strength capable of standing up to Atlantic gales with no more equipment than pick, shovel, sheerlegs and wheelbarrow demands admiration. The plans in the library at Windsor Castle show it to have been furnished with many buildings above and cellars below and to have carried about thirty guns, twenty of which pointed out to sea while the remainder enfiladed the bay. Apart from its commercial advantages the Mole, even incomplete, was now strong enough to deal with any attempt to seize Tangier from the sea. As an insulting afterthought the Dutch man-of-war, taken by Captain Harmon, was filled with cement and sunk at the seaward end.

It was a moment when security was more than ever to be desired, for one of the great decisions in European history, a decision that settled the shape of the continent for a century and a half, was under close study. King Louis XIV was, beyond comparison, the most powerful of the world's rulers. In the prime of life and with the guidance of men whose minds were of the best quality, he commanded an army that had no peer and a navy so improved that it might have justly claimed to be the world's biggest and best. After the peace of February 1674 England and the Dutch Republic patched up their differences but each had so mauled the other that their fleets were shadows of the massed squadrons that had slugged it out in the North Sea. Tempers, however, had not yet cooled to an extent that made any alliance a serious possibility; the ninety years since Alva's reign of terror in the Netherlands were now far enough below the horizon to keep Holland friends with Spain in her genteel poverty and the heavy Dutch warships combined with the galleys of Cartagena to keep up a naval presence in the Mediterranean. There is a powerful current that sits at all times between the Pillars of Hercules which made a wind from a westerly direction essential to get a square-rigger through the Gut of Gibraltar and it was common for this short passage to take days as ships drifted about waiting for the chance to dash or creep through the corridor as the wind might allow. Tangier, happily placed in point of wind and tide, could be a better base for any snapper up of maritime trifles even than Jean Bart's Dunkirk and the friendship of the Lord of Tangier was more than just desirable to the owners of ships from the outside seeking to come in. The thought may very well have occurred to King Louis and to Colbert. The navies of France already had their two main bases at Brest and Toulon, and the squadrons from Brest seeking to reinforce the latter would have a gauntlet to run.

It was the Mediterranean that was now exercising the minds of France's leaders. In May 1674 the majority of the German states joined with the empire and the Diet declared war on France: Sweden, no longer the Sweden of Gustavus, changed sides and sent troops to their aid. Denmark swiftly joined in with her neighbour, though this did not prevent a Dutch-Danish fleet under de Ruyter from breaking the Swedish navy two years later. In northern waters the French fleet did no better than retain a rough equality with its enemies but prospects in the south were brighter. In July 1674, the Sicilians revolted against their Spanish rulers and staged a modified form of Vespers in reverse. The two clients, Spain and Sicily, appealed for help to their friends, the United Provinces and France. The Dutch grudgingly sent a squadron past Tangier, no longer a danger since the Peace, and battleship and galley linked up in strange partnership somewhere off Malaga. French troops landed in Sicily taking the port of Agosta and for a year both navies succeeded in avoiding each other. It was not until January 1676 that they met off the volcano of Stromboli where Duquesne and de Ruyter, in vile weather, pounded away at each other; both fleets were badly hammered but there was no obvious victory for either. When the next encounter came in April off Agosta, the day belonged beyond argument to France and de Ruyter was taken to Palermo to die. A fresh Dutch squadron was met by the triumphant French off Cadiz and was scattered. Only France now maintained a fleet in being in the Middle Sea.

It was then that the historic decision was made. Of all the men who have lived in this world few have been endowed with the intellect of Leibnitz. On his own initiative he had drawn up a memorial for his sovereign which set out the manner in which France, whose only friends now were Bavaria, Hanover and Wurtemburg, might become master of the known world and of much that was still unknown. He expounded the principle that France was far stronger than she might appear and that her enemies were by comparison weaker. Weakest of all, and ripest for pillage, was the Empire of Turkey. 'The conquest of Egypt, that Holland of the East is infinitely easier than that of the United Provinces', promisingly ran the Memorial.

> War with Holland will probably ruin the new Indian com-
> panies as well as the colonies and commerce lately revived
> by France and will increase the burdens of the people while
> diminishing their resources. The Dutch will retire into their

maritime towns, stand there on the defensive in perfect safety, and assume the offensive on the sea with great chance of success. If France does not obtain a complete victory over them, she loses all her influence. In Egypt, on the contrary, a repulse, almost impossible, will be of no great consequence, and victory will give the dominion of the seas, the commerce of the East and of India, the preponderance in Christendom and even the Empire of the East on the ruins of the Ottoman power. The possession of Egypt opens the way to conquests worthy of Alexander; the extreme weakness of the Orientals is no longer a secret. Whoever has Egypt will have all the coasts and islands of the Indian Ocean. It is in Egypt that Holland will be conquered; it is there she will be despoiled of what alone renders her prosperous, the treasures of the East.

Leibnitz may have underrated the Turks, for within less than ten years a Turkish army was at the gates of Vienna and was only driven off at the last moment by the Polish King John Sobieski. Nevertheless his plan was probably capable of execution. There was no Nelson and no Royal Navy to bring down such an expedition and the Maison du Roi and the Regiment of Picardy could have won a battle of the Pyramids with as much ease as did Napoleon. The French of King Louis' day were great builders of canals and Suez should not have been beyond their powers. The King's problem was the antithesis of that of Alexander. There were not too few worlds to conquer: the arrival of a New World meant that there were too many.

Unlike his cousin of England, however, he knew nothing of ships or the sea. Had he been the experienced yachtsman who sailed his own little ships in all weathers he might have drastically changed history, but King Louis was a landsman through and through. Had he turned to the East instead of to the West his grandson Philip might have become Pharaoh of Egypt rather than King of Spain and John Churchill might have gone down in history as no more than an untrustworthy courtier. Certain it is that succeeding English governments, lacking Gibraltar, would have kept the public purse open to maintain a naval base in the top left-hand corner of Africa.

Knowing nothing of these great matters the molemen toiled on, fierce sun, gales and rain tormenting their aching backs. Chest after chest slowly took shape, hardened and, when a flat calm came, was coaxed laboriously into place. The garrison, unpaid, underfed, under-equipped and often in little more than rags, maintained their soldierly discipline, mounted their guards and regularly posted their outlying piquets. Young men of good family with a taste for adventure that fell short of languishing for years in India still found Tangier the place to learn soldiering and to prove their manhood. All armies need a Tangier, a North-West Frontier, or even an Ulster. Lacking these, the soldier approximates more and more to the civilian and tends to substitute civilian ways of thought for his own better values. With the best will in the world, however, life in a starveling garrison, beleaguered though it was, could never have the attractions of buying a pair of colours and going to the Peninsula; Tangier gained some useful subalterns but the place to learn mastery of *la grande guerre* was with Turenne. Young Mr Churchill was one of the few pupils to attend both schools.

8
Mid Term

Charles's Chest, 2,000 tons of masonry, cement, timber and iron, was
at last worked into position and sunk in its place during July 1677.
Within a matter of days two smaller chests, one of half the size of
Charles and the other about a third, were likewise heaved and shoved
out in turn to be sunk and three more were nearly ready to join
them. All this activity around Whitby had not gone unnoticed –
nothing that the Tangier garrison did ever went unnoticed – and the
Moors set themselves to undo as much of the work as they could.

On 17 July they turned out in force, some 500 horse and about
the same number of foot, to ambush the molemen between Devil's
Drop and Whitby itself. Palmes Fairborne by now knew the mind
of the enemy as well as did any Moor and was ready to deal with a
stroke so obvious. The garrisons were watchful and well drilled.
Only about forty assailants managed to get between the two positions and they were smartly driven out, the garrisons taking only
three casualties. Fairborne was himself waiting in ambush to deal
with the Moorish foot as they retreated – to try anything against
the horse would have been like grasping at smoke – but he seems
to have been tapped on the shoulder by his guardian angel just as
he was about to mount. 'I thank God my good genius withheld me,
mistrusting some such thing by the boldness of the attempt' was
how he himself put it. His instinct was sound. The Moors, apparently not really expecting to surprise the vigilant sentries, had put
their faith in luring Fairborne into a rash pursuit and were waiting
for him in force in a place on Teviot's Hill called Blaney's Bottom.

When he did not oblige by walking into their trap the Moorish horsemen demonstrated angrily between Charles Fort and Henrietta Redoubt and a few of their saddles were emptied by musket shot. Fairborne's instinct had become a valuable asset to the garrison and respect for him rose even higher.

It was an uneasy summer and every soldierly quality was needed in the lieutenant-governor. A man in Captain Trelawny's troop died of spotted fever early in July and the dreaded word plague was bandied about. As a precaution Fairborne sent home a demand for more men as 'if the plague comes many will be swept away'. The requisition was met with the customary lack of enthusiasm and no men came; happily nor did the plague, at least not with any great severity. Moors and fever, however, did not add up to the sum of Fairborne's difficulties, for the garrison was suffering one of its intermittent bouts of *le cafard*. On the last day of July it boiled over into mutiny. Captain Carr, who does not seem to have merited a favourable confidential report, touched it off at guard mounting on 31 July. When the drums were ordered to begin one man was late with his stroke; Carr promptly hit him. The drummer, almost as a reflex action, put his hand on his sword but did not draw. Captain Carr, realising that he had made a fool of himself, left matters there but the story inevitably reached Fairborne who was having nothing of that kind in his garrison. The drummer was placed under close arrest and a Court Martial was hastily convened to try both him and a sentry caught asleep at his post. Each was convicted; there was some sympathy for the provoked drummer but none at all for the sentry. The two were sentenced to hang; Fairborne, however, did not have so many soldiers that he could afford to have them killed off by their own people and he commuted the sentences to a form of going through the motions. Each man stood at the foot of the gallows with the rope around his neck nicely adjusted so that he had to remain on tip-toe until he was reckoned punished enough. Ensign Hughes, convicted of drunkenness, was luckier; a public apology at the head of the regiment left him at duty with a lesson on which to ponder. More than one young officer learnt the virtues of sobriety by being cashiered and put to work on the Mole, the worst cases being in chains; there are instances of some of these victims gaining their commissions back by fighting in the ranks with extreme bravery. Palmes Fairborne kept good discipline but he was as fair as he was hard. This was what his soldiers expected of him, and what they both wanted and needed. Of a man who could smell an ambush as he could – and that summer the Moors tried many times to lure the garrison out – much could be forgiven.

Numbers were getting low again with the usual steady trickle of casualties and August was the traditional month for stocking up with men and provender against the winter when landings would be at best difficult and at worst impossible. When it was learned that Sir John Narborough was on his way with 209 recruits, a good store of rations and even some money there was a moment of something like jubilation. It did not long endure. The men were 'very sad creatures, some old men and two of them women in men's clothes'; the provisions almost vanished when Sir John deducted from them six weeks' rations for his sailors to cover the return voyage and although he brought pay for fifteen months there still remained twenty-one more months of arrears. When the navy left the shelter of the Mole it took with it the tiresome Captain Carr and presumably the two transvestites, of whose adventures during their brief stay the record tells nothing[13]. In accordance with orders brought by Narborough, the lieutenant-governor ordered the expulsion of all Jews in Tangier, giving them three months in which to wind up their affairs. Nobody wanted them. To the Moors they were hardly less objectionable than to the Spaniards; their expulsion by Ferdinand and Isabella was clearly warmly approved by generations of Spaniards, for one of the conditions later to be written into the Treaty of Utrecht by which Gibraltar was granted to Queen Anne contained a flat prohibition on any Jew being permitted to reside there. The prohibition still exists, ignored for many years now only because Spain lacked means to enforce it.

The routine of garrison life was broken in October 1677 by a splendid spectacle. Under the walls of Tangier sailed a Turkish thirty-eight-gun ship which was immediately tackled by the British frigate *Portsmouth*, a vessel of half her strength. To the cheers of soldiers, molemen and burgesses *Portsmouth* banged away at her opponent and Captain Canning laid his ship alongside to board. The Turks fought hard, as Turks always do, and it was not until Canning, his lieutenant and thirty of his crew were dead with another forty wounded that she struck. When *Portsmouth* had towed her in the Turk was found to have 150 of her crew dead, including the captain, a renegade German. Her stores came in very useful. Some of the captured powder was traded with the merchants of Cadiz in exchange for beef, a mark of the straits to which Fairborne had been reduced. It was not the fault of the Tangier Commission this time for seventeen English ships, including the victualler *Pioneer*, had lately been captured by Algerian pirates and carried off to Sallee.

The Admiral's reputation as a sea fighter was formidable and had been gained over most of the oceans of the world. In 1666 Captain Narborough had fought the long battle against van Tromp and de Ruyter where he carried on the tradition of Blake under whom he had learnt his trade in Cromwell's Dutch war. Three years later he had attempted without success to open up trade with Peru; his ship, pleasingly called *Sweepstakes*, had been chivvied away from Valdivia by the Spaniards, and there was nothing to show for a long voyage but some more cartographical information about the Magellan Straits. Narborough arrived home in time to take a hand in the battle off Southwold usually called Solebay where his gallantry and professional skill brought him knighthood and flag rank. In the following year, 1673, his squadron had been sent into the Mediterranean to show the teeth of Christendom to the Barbary corsairs and in this enterprise he had had better luck than was to attend those who took on the same adversaries during the next century and a quarter. Narborough sailed into Tripoli, as the Americans Dale and Morris were to try to do in 1802 with lamentable results; after a few broadsides the Dey came to heel. Sir John sailed home with 80,000 dollars in his chest and all the Christian captives helping work his ships. The Algerians now were to hear the guns of the navy of the Restoration, a navy whose fine quality has become shadowed both by the greater triumphs still to come and by its own unseemly interest in making money by devious ways. Narborough blazed the trail for Lord Exmouth, bombarding the town of Algiers and picking up five of the frigates that had been harrying the Tangier victuallers for so long. The relief felt by the garrison was immediate. Narborough's name still figures on the map as an island in the Galapagos to which he had bequeathed it during his South Sea voyage.

In spite of the temporary relief there was no denying that Tangier was not prospering as many had hoped. The Mole was making a fine harbour of it but neither the Levant Company nor anybody else showed signs of interest in it as a seat of an entrepôt trade. Whitby was now well protected by a complicated line of entrenchments joining Charles Fort to the main walls by the tower and extending south to the Henrietta Redoubt. Only between that point and the tiny Devil's Drop post on the seashore remained vulnerable to sudden attack.

For the moment, however, guns and powder still being lacking, the Moors maintained pressure in the old style. Early in the morning of 6 January 1678, while it was still dark, heavy firing suddenly erupted in a great semi-circle all along the western flank. Soon it was plain that this was no mere nuisance but a heavy and determined attack on Charles, Henrietta, Kendall, Pond and Ann forts. Fairborne, watching from the walls, soon sized up the situation. The Moors, in another triumph of hope over experience, wanted him to bring out his troops from behind the walls and were waiting, carefully concealed, to ambush the relievers as soon as there was light enough for them to set out to help the tiny garrisons. Fairborne was having none of that. If the choice had to be made, as it had to be, it was better to let the forts go under than to have his small army caught in the open and destroyed. For three hours his striking force lay under arms, watching helplessly as Kendall blew up and a light appeared on Henrietta suggesting that it too had gone under. As dawn came he moved out with a strong in-lying picket under Captain Leslie, keeping firmly together and taking back the lost works one at a time. Slowly and with every precaution he advanced first on the nearest position, Henrietta; no enemy appeared but the worst fears were realised. The little fort was in ruins, all the garrison being accounted for; two corpses lay amongst the wreckage and the remaining eight had apparently been carried off. The picket moved on, even more warily, driving off by disciplined musketry some 500 horsemen who were lying in wait for them. At Kendall they encountered the same sight. The fort was wrecked and in the remains lay the bodies of the ten men who had held it, some killed outright and others burnt to death. Amongst them lay 'a very valued Sergeant who had been in command of the Fort since it was built'. The only gun, a Portuguese falconet, had been carried away, to be triumphantly paraded through Meknes by Muley Ismail. The remaining forts had managed to hold their ground, though with great difficulty. The Moors were now apparently seeking arms and instructors from the Turks, for the inquest showed them to have developed a new plan of assault. This had been encountered before but not 'great wooden forks which they use to lift them over the fort wall, and also to rear ladders, and which they made use of at both forts in their late successes', as Fairborne explained in his next report. Against such weapons as these only the biggest forts were safe, he explained, and added the usual plea for more men; quality was as important as numbers, for many of the recent recruits were so useless as to be 'past all recovery'. With his usual patience Sir Palmes set to work to rebuild Henrietta and Kendall and to render them as far as possible impervious to repeated attacks of the same kind. How exactly the garrison set about the task is not clear but the ingenuity of the Tangier soldiers was boundless and within a month Fairborne was reporting them safe from further assault of this kind.

What was most worrying was the fact that Muley Ismail seemed to have acquired friends who were capable of changing the entire situation. The Turks were in a class by themselves as professional besiegers. The art had not changed all that much in 200 years since they had stormed Constantinople and, in the last century, both

Malta and Vienna had been very near to going down. In 1669 Candia in Crete had fallen, literally, as their sappers had thoroughly undermined it without any help from a battering-train. All the garrison could do was to watch and pray and get such intelligence as it could. To be compelled to trade powder for victuals was not helpful but at times it could not be avoided. Turkey could claim with justice that the quarrel was hers also. Early in February the garrison was cheered up by the sight of a running battle between the frigates *Chatham* and *Woolwich* and a large Turkish ship, which ended with the Turk being brought prisoner into Tangier roads along with a convoy of twenty-four merchantmen. The Turkish seamen, with admirable spirit, broke out of prison while the garrison was at church, re-took their ship and got her under sail. The Mole batteries opened up and hit her so hard that she ran ashore with the loss of most of the crew. Her wreck was still there a month later when HMS *Foresight* arrived bearing food, ammunition and six months pay off the arrears. A few good meals worked wonders but a nagging worry remained amongst the senior officers.

The seizure of the ship was not a matter of great moment but it may well have put ideas into Turkish heads. Kara Mustafa had come to the throne in 1676 and he was a man with a vision. By degrees he was disengaging from the interminable wars with the Cossacks along the Dnieper and was turning his eyes to the west, to the Hapsburg lands, and his army had become the most formidable under a single command in the whole of Europe. Dalmatia, Hungary, and Vienna itself seemed prizes within the bounds of the possible and once they had fallen it would be time to return to Malta and make the Mediterranean a sea entirely dominated by the crescent flag. Such a natural ally was to be cultivated by any Mohammedan prince who sought to storm the works of the city of Tangier. Fortunately for the garrison, they too had allies. First was the chronic inability of Muley Achmet and Muley Ismail to do other than fight each other for hegemony; second was the plague which in the summer of 1678 spread rapidly from Algiers to Tetuan. Tangier did not escape it but fairly decent sanitation had its reward and deaths were not many. In the hinterland, however, it slew thousands or even tens of thousands.

Lord Inchiquin stepped ashore in May and Sir Palmes Fairborne went home for a well-deserved rest. The Moors celebrated his departure by becoming a little more 'insolent and adventurous'; a party of soldiers sent to cut grass for forage was attacked outside Charles Fort, the assailants using the cover given by the lush summer growth to crawl up to them. Two sentries were cut down but the remainder scuttled back to the fort in time. A fortnight later 200 horsemen lay in ambush between the quarry and the eastern tower in the hope of cutting up the molemen. This time their intelligence failed them, for the molemen were away getting another completed chest into position and the only casualty was an unlucky fisherman. The watchful sentinels spotted what was afoot and delighted molemen paused from their back-breaking work to watch the guns tearing into the cavalry with grapeshot; their marksmanship was good and the survivors fled in a rout. There were no more attacks from that quarter for the rest of the year.

All the same, Tangier was not flourishing. The returns for 1679 show that the sum total of its European inhabitants came only to 2,225, of whom 287 were women, 342 children and twenty were classified as 'Church-men and Priests'. The army accounted for fifty officers and 1,231 other ranks, the Trained Bands contributed 261 effectives and there were eighty-eight of the molemen. Exactly how the troops were organised at this point is not clear but if allowance is made for an adequate number of gunners and their attendant acolytes the number left could hardly muster more than one battalion of the original regiment, the Tangier foot. Whether or not they deserved their reputation of being mainly Papist is impossible to say, but no better troops have ever served their sovereign. By no means all their deeds are recorded but one skirmish, that took place on 3 April 1679, gives a taste of their quality.

Whitby was always the vulnerable spot and the Moors knew it. The governor of Alcazar, Alcaid Omar Ben Haddo, gathered together a force of some 4,500 foot with 600 horse waiting to exploit their success and made an all out attack. Two small wooden block-houses took the shock of the first wave. One of them, described in the *London Gazette* as:

> a low house with a little towere at one end of it, held a sin-
> gle sergeant and twenty-eight men to face the sea of sword
> and spearmen.

After they had resisted as long as they could, they retreated to the tower and blew up the house with 50 or 60 Moors who were upon the roof. They defended themselves for over an hour when, one end of the tower falling in, the Moors entered and found only eight alive with the sergeant, who, refusing to take quarter, were all killed.

At the other redoubt, which was defended by a sergeant and twelve men, the attackers were fought off by musketry until it became impossible to reload, whereupon 'they defended themselves with their swords and half-pikes till some were killed, others wounded and all their arms broken in pieces'. At that point this splendid sergeant, whose name has not come down, ordered those capable of movement to retire while he stayed behind to blow up the fort, 'perishing with the 40 Moors that had entered'. The regiment lost twenty killed and fifteen, all wounded, were taken prisoner; per-haps mercifully, we do not know what happened to them after that. The Moors admitted to 150 killed, though camp gossip doubled that number. It was also commonly believed, probably with good reason, that the attack had been made possible by commercial gentlemen from England who had smuggled some 1,500 barrels of powder to the enemy. After the fight a sixty-day truce was arranged.

Apart from this battle, 1679 was a more tranquil year in the city than it was in England. The 'Popish Plot', the 'Exclusion Bill', 'Habeas Corpus' and the 'Meal Tub Plot' diverted men's minds from the plight of their soldiers. King Charles, however, always kept his faith in the colony's future, possibly because he was at pains never to cause more hurt to Queen Catherine than that furnished by his other passions. On 7 April a Bill was introduced into the Commons 'for annexing Tangier to the Imperial Crown of England'; three days later, as a counter-blast against those who were quietly mooting an effort to sell the place to King Louis, the resolution 'That this House is of opinion that those who shall advise His Majesty to part with Tangier to any Foreign Prince or State, or be instrumental therein, ought to be accounted enemies to the King and Kingdom', passed without a discordant voice. The King waited for the opening of Parliament on 21 October before making his contribution; in a speech dealing with the alliance he had just concluded with Spain and Holland, he spoke very firmly of the need to save his colony. It was all very heartening but it provided neither men, money nor the things that only money could buy. Nothing but the skill and discipline of an unpaid and half-starved body of British soldiers kept this foothold in Africa while the molemen pressed steadily on with a splendid work of engineering that should have been the wonder of the age. The last drawing sent home bears the date 14 November 1679. With its length of more than a quarter of a mile out to sea, its width averaging about thirty-five yards, its height of eighteen feet above low water and its compacted mass of 2,843,280 cubic feet (or 167,251 tons), it was done. The Moorish assaults were now becoming more formidable and more frequent. Whitby had to be abandoned and Tangier stood to arms once more.

Muley Ismail had reached an accommodation with his domestic foes, had digested the lessons of nearly twenty years and was going to wipe the Christians from the face of the earth, cost what it might. His emissaries to Kara Mustafa had plainly earned their pay, for he now had the kind of military mission that has since become a commonplace with African countries. No more would horsemen charge walls; his Turkish Cretan miners would see to it that the walls would first fall down and then the sheer weight of numbers would make short work of those who still survived and offered resistance.

On 25 March 1680 ground was broken and the siege of Tangier began in earnest. Charles and Henrietta Forts, together with the Devil's Drop, were surrounded by seas of coloured burnouses, 'multitudes of horse and foot', and were cut off from the town. The only communication left was by speaking trumpet, with messages usually passed in Irish. Inchiquin sent what relief he could, one weak company under a subaltern, but all they could do was cut their way to Charles and add themselves to the garrison. During the night the Turks and the Moors were busy at their engineering work and dawn showed a line of defended posts between Kendal, Pond and Charles, the most westerly of all the outworks. Cannon fire and musketry were played on the besiegers, but almost without effect. Slowly and inexorably the trench lines moved forward, right under the walls of Pond and Kendal and to within half a musket shot of Henrietta and Charles. By Sunday, 28 March, deep trenches cut Charles from Henrietta and another line ran southward to sever Pond Fort from all assistance. By way of reply the garrison erected a 'cavalier', a platform thirty feet high and capable of holding eight or nine musketeers who were thus able to fire down into the trenches. On the following Wednesday afternoon eight flags of different colours went up from the besiegers' lines. Their significance was not obvious but Captain Trelawny, from Charles Fort, shot down two of them upon which all were removed. On 5 April, as the trench lines were curving round, completely severing the western forts from the town, and strange-wheeled engines whose purpose nobody knew lumbered into sight, Sir Palmes Fairborne disembarked. His presence was as good as a fresh battalion but could not dispel the fear that these new activities had brought with them.

Fairborne took these developments far more seriously than did Lord Inchiquin. His report to Williamson made a week after his return told how he had found the Moors

> entrenched between Charles and Henrietta Forts and the town and with a treble trench deep and broad, at least 20 feet, with several places of arms within their trenches; avenues from each to succour one another upon any sally which we should make against them, so formidable and so regular that no Christian enemy ever proceeded better or more resolutely.

The governor was less worried; the two main forts held 240 men, victualled for five months and tolerably well munitioned. Only Fairborne spotted that a line was being directed under Fort Charles and had the news shouted across in Erse. Captain Trelawny, unperturbed, set to work countermining and a grim little battle was fought in the bowels of the earth, ending with the discomfiture of the miners.

On Easter Sunday, 11 April, the expected attack came in against the weaker position, Henrietta. Lieutenant Wilson with his sergeant and thirty men fought like heroes. The wheeled engines which had puzzled so many turned out to be galleries, standard siege works in antiquity and still not useless, which were trundled under the walls to facilitate the throwing of stinkpots. Wilson's men set about them with musket shot and grenades, the stormers fled and some bold spirits nipped down and burnt the machines to ashes. In another place an attempt was made to mine the wall by erecting long booms, covering them with faggots and using them for shelter as the pick and shovel men went to work. Again the heavy musket balls tore into them and a few brave men slid down ropes to put them to the torch. As the attackers drew off, Wilson defiantly embellished his fort with two Moors' heads on a pole. It was a heartening success but it suggested worse things to come.

Sir Palmes went back to his accustomed occupation of writing begging letters home. The unused Mole funds must be re-allocated to the town fortifications 'or it will be too late'. He needed men and arms – 'not one spare arm in the stores except a few blunderbusses' – and he never saw a place more ruinous, 'not one thing being in a condition fit for defence'. The Moors continued their elaborate digging, protecting the work with Sangars in true North-West Frontier style.

Trelawny manufactured a mortar which could lob grenades into the trenches, probably the original *minenwerfer*, but it could only be of nuisance value. The fort garrisons, knowing well that Fairborne had no field force with which to drive off the besiegers, set their teeth and waited. The prospect before them was not an attractive one but they had to endure it. Fairborne, as determined as Clive would be always to show a bold front to a primitive enemy, kept up his patrols as far as Pole Fort and Norwood Redoubt, digging a covered way between them; in front of Peterborough Tower, to which the survivors of a fallen Charles Fort would have to make their way or from which any sally might erupt, he put lines of palisades. The underemployed in the town were put to work 'making fire-works and fitting hand grenades'. Devil's Drop, the fortlet on the beach west of Whitby, had to be temporarily abandoned as it was now untenable completely surrounded by trenches on all sides but the sea.

Almost as worrying as the new tactics and weapons was an apparent change in the type of soldier now being employed by the besiegers. Years of familiarity with the Moors had caused the English to regard them as noisy show-offs whose military capacity was pretty contemptible. Suddenly a large proportion of them were ebony-black foot soldiers who were game to stand and fight rather than gallop off at the first glimpse of serious danger. These blacks were Sudanese, Dinkas and Shilluks, slaves or descendants of slaves who feared no man and almost enjoyed a fight for its own sake. Nobody knew what gods they honoured, if indeed they honoured any, for they were certainly not Muslims and it was something of a shock to find them willing to serve their hated masters. By some means, however, they had been enlisted and they were an enemy that nobody could despise. Two centuries later the same kind of men were to form the backbone of the army which Kitchener took to Omdurman. Probably they were first pressed into service as mere diggers, for at this work they excelled, but compelled their own promotion by their steadiness under fire and their manifest bravery in a fight.

Fairborne learnt of them after their first near-success on 29 April. Signals from Pole Fort, which had a good view to the west, suggested that something was going on around Charles Fort. Fairborne rode out at once to Pole in order to see for himself and the sight presented to him was alarming. Great numbers of the enemy were busy in the valley to the east of Teviot's Hill, about a quarter of a mile to the west of Charles and defiladed from it by another, smaller hill. Officers were bustling about from one party to another, small figures could be seen lugging timber and stones and the only possible conclusion was that this was the entrance to a good-sized mine. When, after a couple of hours, something like 200 black soldiers could be made out taking up positions in the trenches, it was plain that a breach was expected and these were to be the stormers. Then, very suddenly, a flag of truce went up and was answered from the fort. Only later did Fairborne learn what happened. Two Europeans, a renegade Englishman and a Frenchman from Tetuan, were taken blindfolded inside and were interviewed by Captain Trelawny and Captain St John. They explained that the fort was undermined and the men of the Tangier Regiment could take their choice between slavery or being blown to pieces. According to the record Trelawny told the traitor that 'he could do his worst and that the garrison was sent to hold the Fort, not to surrender it'. Probably he put it more robustly than that but the reply deserves to stand with Nicholson's at Calais. 'Take that to your German General'. The renegades withdrew, to be sent straight back with a demand that Trelawny see for himself the plight he was in. Two miners descended the shaft and came back to report that the story was true. Trelawny returned the same answer, his musketeers opened up, to be joined by 'a pounding from the great gun' and the hoisting of every flag they possessed. At 8 a.m. Fairborne, from the roof of Pole Fort, felt the place rocked by an explosion and Charles was blotted out in cloud of black smoke. As it cleared, however, he could see that the walls still stood and he was 'saluted with three ring-ing cheers as a sign that all was well'. During this excitement one Moor broke away and sped towards the town as fast as his legs would take him. A patrol picked him up and brought him to the governor. His reason for deserting seemed good – he was wanted for murder – and he was willing to talk. The strength of the Moorish army was 'all the country could afford, beside some thousands of the king's army of blacks. The Moors had lost so many men in the attack on Henrietta that the word had gone out saying that from now on there would be no more attempts at escalades but that each fort in turn should be reduced by mining. Confirmation of the truth of his story came the following day in a letter from the Alcaid. The Emperor, it asserted, 'had subdued all his enemies at his heart's desire and is returned in peace to his house'. As for the Alcaid, it had been commanded not to return from Tangier until he had taken all the forts and 'although the mine has failed once, another time it will take effect and that he was there for a long life or a short one but he would carry out the King's behest'. Fairborne returned a stern answer but, as both of them knew, he was whistling in a graveyard. The little forts had not been constructed to cope with this sort of attack and the only choice to be made was between voluntary evacuation or a spectacular end.

Henrietta was the feeblest of the works. On 8 May the Moors were seen hauling a gun on to a hill nearby and soon they began a steady cannonade. The gun was only a 2 1/2-pounder, taken some time before from Fort Ann (which had been abandoned), but it was sufficient for its purpose. The next day Henrietta's commander was under the bitter necessity of shouting to Trelawny that the walls were crumbling, that the building was mined and that the end was very near. Charles passed the message in the same way to the town and Fairborne, at his wits' end to know what to do for the best, decided in conference with Lord Inchiquin to try and negotiate a surrender. The Alcaid took a high tone. Why, with the fort in his hands, should he be expected to offer any terms at all? To that there was no answer but it was unthinkable that a platoon of British soldiers should be tamely handed over to captors who would work them almost to death and then smash them into the foundations of their walls. As the State Papers put it, 'this [surrender] not suiting the temper of the English was at once refused'. Fairborne set to work to scrape together some sort of relief column. For once he had a small stroke of luck. Vice-Admiral Herbert was in the port; his private life was a scandal even by Restoration standards but Herbert was a fighter. From his ships he found 100 seamen to take over the defences of the Mole, leaving Fairborne to pick the best and fittest of his soldiers for their task, to rescue a handful of men from the midst of a Moorish army now swollen to about 5,000. The most he could muster was 480 men.

The worst had not yet come. When Trelawny shouted through his trumpet that Charles in turn had become impossible to hold any longer – the damage done by the mine must have been greater than realized for the walls were now crumbling – he had to be believed and the task of saving both was beyond any man's power with the tiny force available. Between 8–9 p.m., 12 May, Henrietta surrendered and the survivors could be seen being whipped on their way by a full thousand exultant Moors. Next morning, in the early hours, an explosion carried away most of the building. Whether it was Moors' work or whether the brave sergeant had left a slow fuse to the remains of his powder will never be known. The capitulation added a further hazard to Charles Fort, for an Irishman from Henrietta, who had heard and understood all the speaking-trumpet messages, 'was forced to betray what he knew of their intention to force their way out'.

Charles was indeed to be given up, at 7 a.m. the next morning. Trelawny's garrison of 176 and 'Captain Trelawny's little boy' were going to have their work cut out to make their way through the three lines of trenches crammed with the enemy if ever they were to get to the safety of the Upper Castle some 700 yards away. Promptly on the stroke the gate was opened and the grenadiers under Captain St John rushed for the first trench. As the leading men reached it, Ensign Richards fired the two-inch train leading to the last of the powder. As St John rushed the first trench, Fort Charles went up with a roar. Towards them, from the town, came the forlorn hope of Fairborne's relief force, Captain Hume, two subalterns and eighty-four men of the recently arrived Scotch companies, the main body of about 150 men under Major Boynton following 150 yards behind them. 100 yards behind again marched the reserve, in a column six deep, made up of Captain Muneresh and another 112 men. A flank guard of seventy under Captain Leslie covered the seaward side above the now-deserted Whitby.

The fort garrison, now closed up into one block, fought its way through a solid mass of Moors, hacking and stabbing with sword and half-pike since their muskets were useless. Fairborne saw them go down into the second trench, from which a heaving, yelling mass slowly emerged.

It was in the third trench that the fight became most furious. This was the widest and the deepest, twenty-four feet across and fourteen from top to bottom, slippery and muddy after recent rain. Here, in a welter of blood, the garrison of Fort Charles was obliterated. Of the 176 who went into this grave 124 never emerged alive. The gallant Trelawny was cut to pieces as he scrambled up the bank to try and save his little son; the boy and fourteen wounded men were carried off to Meknes, only St John, two subalterns named Clause and Roberts and thirty-six men managing to fight their way clear. Even then their troubles were not over. The main body and reserve of the relief column, out in the open, were broken by the sheer numbers of their assailants, who had charged in behind the forlorn, and were put to flight. Only the superb courage of Captain Hume, who fought like a wounded bull, kept the last party together and when he went down, knocked over by a Moorish horseman (who 'was at once despatched'), it was St John who took over. The remnant of the Fort Charles men faced about and, weary though they were, fought off the hordes of enemy for long enough to see the sadly reduced party over the last ditch and into the castle. St John was one of the last to be wounded by a bullet that lodged in his side but he managed to make his way to safety. Admiral Herbert sent boats to take off the fourteen men in Devil's Drop, under heavy fire; only one man could swim and the rest preferred captivity to drowning. They probably lived long enough to regret their choice. Twenty-two seamen were killed in the boats.

Into the city stalked a great terror, terror of a kind to which the people of Byzantium had become accustomed as the Turks crept nearer and nearer but of a depth unknown to the more sheltered English. Charles had been amongst the biggest and best of the outer works; if it could melt away in this fashion there could be no hope for the others and even the curtain of Tangier itself no longer seemed the solid and inexpugnable thing it had been for nearly twenty years. Lord Inchiquin summoned a council of war. 'Some of the members replied [to the Alcaid's hard terms] that considering the enemy's skill in gunnery and mining, they did not think they could last three days; but Sir Palmes and others were for holding out'.

Fairborne had a reputation to sustain; he was not a man to be panicked and he had in his youth fought the Turks in the German wars. The enemy, from being despised as a mere nuisance of tin soldiers who would never stand serious battle, had become what one speaker called 'a puissant and formidable foe'. All the more reason, in Fairborne's judgement, to show a bold face. Our own shaken troops had to be reassured of their superiority and the Moors must on no account be allowed to feel themselves the better men. Once more the Tangier garrison were the first British soldiers to encounter conditions in which cold calculation had to be made whether to die hard or live to fight another day. In due time Sir Colin Campbell would be heard to pronounce it better for him to see every man of the Queen's Guards dead upon his face than that the enemy should see the colour of their knapsacks. In the summer of 1940 similar arguments were heard. There have always been Fairbornes to appear when needed.

It was probably due to his reputation more than anything else that the Alcaid modified his terms when Captain Leslie, Lieutenant Fitzgerald and Mr Loddington arrived at his camp under flag of truce. The Moors, Nubians and Turkish miners had also been hard hit and both sides knew it. Leslie made it very plain that if the Alcaid wanted Tangier now he would have to fight for every redoubt, every stretch of wall, every alleyway and every building. Wisely, the Moor decided that he could afford to wait. A four-month armistice was agreed, the conditions being that Pole and Norwood Forts should be handed over in three days time, that all the others save three should be left within three months; for their part the Moors would dismantle their new batteries and cattle might once more be allowed out to graze in the fields. Leslie and Fitzgerald were shown the mine in course of preparation and 'they were bound to admit that it was as ingeniously carried out as anything they ever saw'. Equally discouraging was the sight of all the guns from Charles and Henrietta neatly unspiked and ready for work. This was something the Moors could never have done unaided. The forts that the garrison were allowed to retain were the ones upon which the continued existence of Tangier depended. Without Fountain there would be no water, since nobody had given much thought to the old supplies so painstakingly described in the book abstracted long ago by Peterborough. The other two, Cambridge and Bridges, were the outposts of Fountain. All the buildings to the south and west were to go. As a number of them are no longer mentioned by name it seems probable that they had already been given up before the great assault. With a total garrison of no more than battalion strength it would hardly have been possible to keep them manned even in peace conditions.

The terms were better than might have been expected but the truth could not be blinked at; unless reinforcements greater by far than anything seen in the last two decades were to arrive, and arrive soon, the occupants of Tangier were tenants at sufferance; at any moment a determined attack would be bound to succeed and the best that any Christian within the walls could hope for was a quick end. Fitzgerald was sent home at once overland with letters for Sir Leoline Jenkins, the secretary, and he needed no bidding not to spare his horses. The only concession made by the Moors was a courteous suggestion that work on the Mole might continue 'which shows that they do not yet think the Mole good enough for them'. Some news of the calamity must have gone ahead, for the Ordnance Minute books for May show substantial quantities of arms and ammunition being made ready for shipping from the tower to the city. Perhaps Whitehall did not deserve all the blame. Pepy's diary entry for 7 May 1669 says 'And so to the Duke of York, having a great mind to speak to him about Tangier; but when I came to it, his interest for my Lord Middleton is such that I dared not'. Pepys did not usually lack moral courage to this extent; probably he knew that nothing he might say would make any difference.

Historians and others have had much to say about the defects in the character of Charles II; whatever his faults may have been, the King was still at heart the young Prince who had fought at Worcester and he had the qualities of a soldier. As soon as the dreadful situation was made plain to him he rose to the occasion and acted like a king. By some means he put his hands on money and issued on 2 June 1680 the Royal Warrant that was the birth certificate of at least one famous regiment. The four Scotch companies that had fought so well during the retreat from Charles were to be reinforced by others and in time they came by the name the Royal Scots. Nor were they all that the King would send.

> The five companies now going out of this Kingdom under the command of John, Earl of Mulgrave, shall have the first place as a battalion of Guards; that the 4 companies of the Scotch regiment with the 4 other companies from Ireland make one battalion and take the rank of the said Scotch regiment, that is to say next after the battalion of Guards; that when the rest of the said Scotch regiment arrive there (with the 4 Scotch and 4 Irish companies already mentioned) make 2 battalions and take rank after the battalion of Guards; that the 12 companies of the Garrison regiment (Tangier) and the 4 English companies sent thither last year make 2 battalions and take rank after those of the Guards and the Scotch regiment.

The despatch of a battalion of his own Household, at a time when he might easily have needed it at home, shows the King's expressed concern for the colony was entirely genuine and does him credit. In addition to this he approached the consul-general of Spain who undertook to move a force of 200 cavalry to Gibraltar and there put themselves under the command of Lord Inchiquin. Lastly he allowed his own bastard, Charles Fitzcharles, son of Catherine Pegg, to go with the expedition.

Lord Inchiquin, after consultation with Fairborne, decided that he could for the moment be of more service in London where he could put all his weight behind the effort to save Tangier. He left early in June and Sir Palmes again became the acting governor. On the last day of the month this hard-pressed man saw some lifting of the

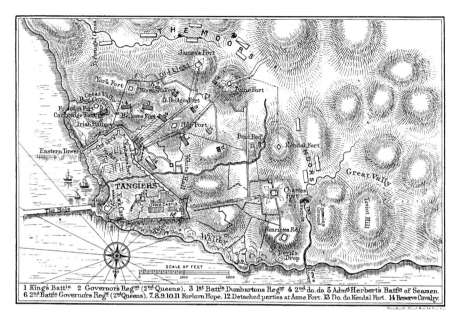

7. The ground and forts round Tangier.

clouds when four ships from Ireland glided under the guns of the
Mole and the first 600 men of Dumbarton's marched ashore. There
would have been more, but the transport *Garland* had sprung a leak
and returned to Kinsale with two companies. Well could he write
that 'I am rejoiced to see so many brave men come over and to
understand His Majesty's resolution to send more, whilst I doubt not
to regain the place and fortify it to His Majesty's satisfaction'. The
Spanish horse moved to Barbate; clearly Fairborne had hardly any
other cavalry for Sir John Lanier, commanding the Tangier horse, had
been packed off to London to plead for more and, inevitably, for
money to pay for those now arriving. Once more the King sup-
ported him and three new troops were at sea by the end of August.
The Guards and most of the foot arrived during the summer, and Mr
Shere applied the Mole funds to fortifications and buildings to house
the men. Pay for the original garrison was not included with the
stores. In August they were owed eighteen months' arrears. The new
arrivals had been paid in advance. To show how seriously he took

Tangier the King appointed the Earl of Ossory, son of the Duke of Ormond, to governorship but before he could take up his appointment he died. Fairborne wrote to Jenkins to say that he welcomed the decision but hoped it would not affect either the £500 he received as commander nor his pension, adding wistfully that things in Tangier were thrice English prices and 'I have been forced to take up money on credit to maintain my table'.

The Alcaid had been watching all this with unconcealed anger. Once upon a time the spectacle would have unnerved him and he would have been only too willing to enter into a treaty of long duration but now he was a far more confident man. His army, in its technical branches, was probably better than Fairborne's, French friends were now abundant as France was Turkey's unspoken ally and he had all the guns, powder and soldiers he could use. On 4 September 1680 he gave fair warning of his intentions. The truce had all but expired and on the rising of the new moon he would consider himself free to strike. During the night of 14/15 September the flags that marked the boundaries were removed and at dawn some guns were fired to mark the new campaigning season.

9

Brigade-sized Battles

By mid–May 1680 the life of every Christian in Tangier hung in the balance. The official records are scrappy, often illegible and not uncommonly in ciphers that now defy unravelling. By good fortune, however, these are supplemented by the accounts of a few men able to write of what they saw. One of these was John Ross, 'gentleman, a sentinell in the Foot Guards'; whose little book called 'Tangier Rescue' appeared a year later. Just this once, and as his spelling was nearer the usual than were most papers of the time he may tell his story as he set it down.

When the glad news came of the arrival of His Majesty's Friggots the Rupert, the Saphire and others with six hundred of His Majesties Guards from England, under the command of Colonel Edward Sackville, a man of most esteemable gifts and parts, With many brave Volunteer Gentlemen, encouraged to undertake this noble enterprise in the service of their King, and country, by that hopeful young youth the Earl of Plymouth (whose mature-fruit did anticipate his years, and antidate his age). This gallant recruit changed the effeminate designs and stupid procedures of the burghers to a more propitious and generous resolution, and did animate the old souldiers to a more qualified gallantry, and courage and so confirmed the resolutions of all, that they thought themselves in a sufficient posture of defence. These Volunteers landed at Tangier, July 2 1680, with 240 of the King's Own Regiment under the command of Colonel Edward Sackville, and one Mr Bowes; a hundred and twenty of the Earl of Craven's Regiment, under the Command of Colonel Tollemach (a gentleman gifted with the acuteness, and flowrish of wit;) a hundred and twenty of the Duke of York's Regiment, under the Command of a modest young gentleman, Captain Fawtry; a hundred and twenty of the Earl of Mowgrave's (Mulgrave's) Regiment, under the command of Captain Kirk, a youth of admirable endowments, according to the politeness of Court. All those with the Volunteers and drafts of the Independent Companies were regimented under the command of Colonel Edward Sackville as their Colonel and were called the King's Battalion. After this Landed the valorous Hacket, Major to that renowned Regiment of the Earl of Dumbriton (Dumbarton), all of them men of approved valour; whose fame echoed the sound of their glorious achievements in France and other Nations, leaving behind them a report of their glorious victories, wherever they came, both at home and abroad, every place witnessing and giving a large testimony of their renown.

The Earl of Mulgrave was the least valuable of the new arrivals, and his reputation for gallantry referred more to the boudoir than the battlefield. By 25 July he was back in Windsor and gave 'His Majesty an account of that place' that he had so briefly adorned. All that remains as evidence of the Earl's activity at Tangier is a bill of 25s for 'a pair of colours of green, white and crimson taffeta with two figures painted in oil'. Command of the Guards devolved upon Colonel Edward Sackville, who was everything that one expects a Guards Colonel to be. Under his eye, and with the vigorous support of the new arrivals, everything tightened itself up.

Such was the new martial spirit about the place that even Mr Shere left his Mole, bought himself a horse and a sword and turned volunteer. Admiral Herbert, who would have to dine out on his Tangier experiences when he got home, was determined to have some worth telling. His naval brigade of 600 cutlasses would be a very serviceable addition to the force at need.

The stores inventories suggest some improvement in the quality of weapons even though it was not great. Of the 1,700 muskets sent to Tangier during the summer 1,000 were matchlocks and the remainder new snaphaunces; the King's Own companies also carried a twelve-inch long plug bayonet; as it was only fixed by jamming its haft into the muzzle it seems unlikely that it could have been used more than once without coming out. Tangier experience may have done something for the development of Marlborough's sovereign weapon, the flintlock musket with ring bayonet. In 1680, from all accounts, the British soldier preferred the butt of his musket for in-fighting and he was probably the best judge. The artillery provided was, however, very poor. Fairborne had asked desperately for heavier pieces and they had been furnished; the trouble was that they seemed to have been cast in a hurry and not uncommonly burst on firing.

Sir Palmes Fairborne accepted battle with a higher heart than he would have believed possible only weeks ago. He had two immediate purposes. First, he wanted elbow-room and that especially towards the vulnerable south-west side; second, he was determined to give Moors, Nubians and Turkish Cretans the hammering of their lives, both to cheer up the garrison and to make future diplomacy less one-sided. At 3 a.m. on 20 September the garrison fell in on the Parade Ground. Mr Ross, though he could hardly have realised that he was about to witness the first appearance of the Brigade of Guards in battle, made note of his commanding officer's brief allocution. Colonel Sackville can hardly have failed to know that much was expected of them. The idea of a special regiment of big men, per-fectly drilled, whose one object was to do everything rather better than the common run of soldiers, to keep at it for longer and above all to do it with a style that suggested effortless superiority was a new one and viewed by the line with some suspicion. Sackville spoke laconically, as a guardsman should, bidding 'his good fellows' to 'keep close according to order, to obey strictly the orders of their officers and to act courageously like the King of England's Guards'.

As the sun rose over their left shoulders, men waited their turn. First, as soon as the gates at the Catherine Port were thrown open, it was the business of the horse. Led by Fairborne himself, with Lord Mordaunt and Mr Shere riding with him, the Tangier horse cantered out into the open, shook itself into line and galloped between the empty trenches to Pole Fort. To their surprise they found it deserted; they signalled the news back to the foot before wheeling to their left and charging off towards Fort Monmouth. The Forlorn Hope, 200 men under Tollemache with the Earl of Plymouth in attendance, doubled smartly across the intervening 400 yards and moved into the empty works. Behind them marched the Guards, bearing a little to the right between Pole and the ruins of Kendal; then the line was extended to the left towards Monmouth, the 1st Tangier Battalion linking up with the Guards and Dumbarton's joining them on their left. Herbert's sailors scampered out the short distance to cover Cambridge while the 2nd Tangier Battalion remained in reserve within the city wall. Some accounts say that a detachment was sent to capture Ann Fort and the author of 'A Particular Account of the late Successes' asserts that Captain Fitzpatrick

> most resolutely and gallantly beat the enemy from a trench (a matter of 40 furlongs beyond his post) which afterwards proved very advantageous for the benefit and safety of the labourers and security for the guard of Pole Fort.

As Ann lay some four furlongs from the Catherine Port it may be that the forty is no more than a copying error. Probably Fitzgerald was sent out with what we should call an officer's fighting patrol to find out the state of play. The horse found Monmouth deserted; Fitzgerald may have found the same thing at Ann. In any event, Ann was never re-occupied.

So far Fairborne seemed to have caught the Moors off balance. Major Beckman, his engineer, soon had his fatigue parties busy around Pole and it was not until their work was well advanced and the labourers were bringing timber and stone from the city in substantial amounts that the enemy came to life. Even then they made no concerted attack, milling about in large numbers in their lines between James and Monmouth but resisting all blandishments to come out and fight. Strong patrols were sent to the old works at the south and west and they succeeded in clearing them out without much difficulty. By about 2 p.m. all firing from the enemy lines stopped and Fairborne's pioneers were able to work unhindered. Six hours later Pole Fort and its trench system were fit to be garrisoned again and the main body marched back into the city. Colonel Sackville and 500 Guardsmen were left to hold the new outpost zone, with Lord Plymouth (whom everybody liked) and the experienced St John to keep him company. It had been a useful day's work. It was repeated the following day, the garrison marching out trailing its coat and the Moors contenting themselves with some artillery play. Casualties so far were only seven killed and eighteen wounded.

Sir Palmes Fairborne knew what he was about. If he performed the same evolution a third time it was a moral certainty that the Moors would be lying up somewhere and would cut in between troops and city as soon as the afternoon withdrawal began. As he expected they ran true to form and were lured into a neat little ambush laid by the musketeers of the Dumbarton's regiment with a few guns. The Moors 'lost heart and turned and ran', leaving their dead behind. Once more casualties in the garrison had been negligible. Next day, however, they appeared in far greater force and a general battle ended with little advantage to either side.

It had all been tolerably satisfactory. Pole Fort, the one place from which an attack could be broken up before reaching the walls, was in strong hands. The enemy had had a good fright and, best of all, the troops had behaved splendidly. Many a tiny fight had taken place in which the horse had shown great dash and determination and the foot patrols were 'very active and daring', says Ross.

The despatch he sent home shows the governor's pleasure. He praised the personal courage of Admiral Herbert, who had been slightly wounded, and spoke highly of his prudent advice and readiness to assist the garrison at all times. Major Beckman, the Swedish-born sapper, was 'not only a valiant and steady man but an able man in his profession'. Colonel Sackville

> hath shown himself a person of experience and valour, as hath Lt. Col. Tollemache, Capt. Kirk, Lieut. Slater, Lieut. Fitzpatrick, and Lieut. Bridgman; and so hath Major Hackett and all the officers of the Earl of Dumbarton's Regt. as also all the officers and soldiers of the standing forces of the Garrison and all the volunteers hath behaved themselves with infinite courage.

A King's son could hardly escape praise, but Fairborne was not the man to say 'he would let no action pass, either on horseback or on foot, when he would not be present' unless he meant it. As for Lord Mordaunt, 'no man was braver, both on horseback and on foot'. Stores were still as short as ever; the 1,700 snaphaunces and matchlocks were still only invoices and 'unless a speedy supply be sent, both of them and iron pots, I must give over fighting, for without the one or the other nothing can be done'.

The Moors, consistent with their new style, decided to smash Pole Fort rather than storm it. Two new batteries went up and heavier guns than any yet seen appeared on the sandhills above Whitby, clearly to keep off any landing from the sea to outflank them. The Spanish horse were brought over from Barbate on 6 October and soon showed that the spirit of El Cid was very much alive. The dash with which they tore into the Moorish harkas was admired by everybody, even by the Tangier horse. The new cavalry from England had been so infamously equipped that they looked 'more like ruinated troopers than men fit for service', but, added Sir Palmes hastily, 'their officers are very good men'. The new guns had nothing to commend them with their rotten carriages and flawed metal. On 9 October one of them blew up, badly injuring St John, wounding Mr Shere in the leg and narrowly missing Sir Palmes and the admiral. The Moorish gunners, on the other hand, were better, even good enough to single out the governor's private house in order to show the Alcaid's displeasure with him.

The first fortnight of October was a time for consolidation of the gains made in the September battles and, despite all the obvious weaknesses, there was a new spirit of cheerfulness abroad. Fairborne undoubtedly ran a tight ship. When Lieutenants Church and Collier, both of the Guards, fought a duel the survivor, Collier, was tried by a jury, convicted of manslaughter and sentenced to be burnt on the hand. This the governor reckoned punishment enough and the offender was returned to duty. Admiral Herbert kept discipline in idiosyncratic fashion. Three years later he got himself into trouble for having his fleet surgeon stripped naked and left with one big toe tied to the cabin roof exposed to the pleasantries of the loose women in whose company his commander delighted.

Amidst all the bustle there came a moment when everything suddenly stopped. Lord Plymouth had picked up an attack of dysentery during his spell in the trenches retaken from the Moors, probably as a result of their filthy condition rather than from the exposure to one night of dirty weather which was assumed to be the cause. After several miserable weeks, on 17 September 1680, he died. The garrison went into mourning, for he had been a popular young man and, being the King's son, he had done much by his mere presence to dispel the 'forgotten army' school of thought which British soldiers far from home are inclined to affect. Charles Mordaunt, his boon companion, accompanied the body home; the Secret Service, whose records are preserved by the Camden Society, paid out £120 for his funeral. He had been just eighteen and one cannot help feeling that Catherine Pegg's son was a better man than that of Lucy Waters. Mordaunt, in a few years time, would be giving substantial help to William of Orange shortly after his arrival at Torbay. Whatever may have happened in past years, Tangier was now no nest of Papists.

Fairborne made a last effort to secure some sort of peace but was not willing to pay the Alcaid's price, the handing back of Pole Fort. As it was plain to see that batteries and mines were nearly ready for an attack on this highly important work, the council of war decided to get in first. In accordance with his usual habits, Sir Palmes went out to have a look at things for himself, taking with him a strong patrol of 150 foot and a troop of Spanish horse. Don Salvador de Monteforte and Fairborne had struck up a friendship and the caballeros plainly got on well with their temporary general. It seems that the Alcaid was determined to rid himself of his most dangerous opponent for it was noticeable that as soon as contact was made nearly all the fire was concentrated on one man. A musket ball hit him in the chest and Sir Palmes fell; this appeared to be the signal for a general attack for parties of Moors sprang everywhere from the earth and rushed towards the fallen man and his escort. Don Salvador and his troopers rode fiercely into them, forcing them back into their trenches under the edges of their sabres until they themselves came under a heavy fire and had to withdraw. As the Moors attempted to follow them the Spanish horse faced about and charged again as their forefathers had done. The Moors could not stand against the Spanish fury and fled: the horse grimly wiped their swords and trotted back unmolested, bringing with them the sorely wounded governor. Dumbarton's, who had provided the infantry, were not heavily engaged but Captain Forbes and half a dozen men were killed.

The command fell on Colonel Sackville, who was fully equal to the task. After a day of preparation the garrison fell in very quietly at 3 a.m. on 27 October; so good was their discipline that, in the words of Mr Shere, 'although the enemy had perdues under our very walls they could not have taken the least alarm'.

Sackville was having no useless mouths in his command. His five battalions of regulars mustered only about 1,500 men and the entire cavalry, English and Spanish, something in the order of 350. Admiral Herbert once more produced his ad hoc Marines and this time other auxiliaries were pressed to create a diversion. The molemen and boys were furnished with drums and makeshift Colours, equipped with all the spare weaponry that could be found and told to provide themselves with everything on four legs that from a distance might look like a horse. This they did with relish and gave a spirited impersonation of a reserve of cavalry. As soon as the main attacking force had left the city, their task – there were about fifty of them – was to march to the spur between Peterborough Tower and Catherine Port, make a great deal of noise and display all the Colours they had. On the other sea flank, beyond the Mole, the navy displayed every man that could be mustered with 'waistcloths and colours', waiting in boats as if they intended a landing on that flank. Both deception plans were to keep large numbers of Moors running up and down expending powder to no purpose. Fairborne, whose plan it was, insisted on being carried there in a litter.

In perfect silence the army moved through Catherine Port and shook itself into line, the Guards on the right, then Dumbarton's, (divided into two battalions), then the Tangier Battalion and with Herbert's sailors on the left. As soon as they were drawn up, Colonel Sackville made his arranged signal and the 150 men of Dumbarton's detailed for the Forlorn Hope doubled out of Pole Fort, followed closely by their own reserve. The Moors in their trenches were far more numerous than anybody had bargained for and a very bloody hand-to-hand fight began. A moment later the whole line advanced and, as usual, Moors and black Sudanese sprang up out of the ground. Soon every battalion was at grips and 'like fire and lightning all went to it at once'. On the right the Guards 'charged and drove back the Moors from the ground whereon they had planted their guns, of which two were captured by them'. Captain Bowes, commanding the battalion, was much criticised afterwards for not moving to the help of Dumbarton's, 'ordering his men to stand to their posts on pain of death'. Apparently he was concerned to get the guns away from danger of recapture and he may well have had the right of it. His own orders were plain and the Scotch got themselves out of trouble by their own efforts.

A sixteen-foot pike is not the ideal weapon for clearing trenches, but it seems to have served. On the other hand bombing from traverse to traverse, a standard drill in 1680, is within the experience of many living men. The grenade of the day was at least as good as any used in 1915. Slowly the whole line went forward, across the new trenches into the old ones on a line between the dismantled James and Monmouth Forts, where the infantry halted. The immediate task of their pioneers was now to bridge these sufficiently to make it possible for the cavalry to cross and complete the victory. This they did with commendable speed and soon the troops of Captain Neatby, Don Salvador and Don Maurique de Moronia were thundering in ragged lines and wedges into the broken enemy. The Moorish horse fought gallantly but they were outweighted and were soon fleeing in uncontrollable rout. All that was left to do was count the dead and assemble the booty. The casualty figures, like those of the numbers engaged on both sides, are not reliably reported anywhere. They were plainly the heaviest so far, for the Tangier Battalion was next day reduced to fifty effectives and the others were probably in no better shape. They rode victorious into the city Fairborne had defended for eighteen long years. As the sun dipped behind what had been Charles Fort, he died, 'a worthy, brave and able officer', as Mr Shere wrote in his diary. The King charged himself with the care of Lady Fairborne and his family and probably found the money – Sir Palmes left hardly any – for the window in Westminster Abbey with its inscription 'Sacred to the immortal memory of Sir Palmes Fairborne, Knight, governor of Tangier, in the execution of which command he was mortally wounded by a shot from the Moors then besieging the town, in the 46th year of his age, October 24th 1680'. Few of those who read it now are even curious enough to wonder what an English knight was doing governing Tangier. He was the first senior officer of the regular army to die in battle and to be buried by his soldiers in the way of Abercromby, Moore and so many others that were to come after. And he was not the least of them.

Nor was he the only member of his family to win renown in campaigns so little rewarding. Palmes Fairborne's eldest son, Stafford, became an officer in the Royal Navy, saw service off the coast of his father's old bailiwick and as acting Captain of HMS *Bonaventure* broke up a squadron of Sallee pirates in June 1685. Stafford Palmes rose high, seeing as much action as any man of his generation and ending up as one of Queen Anne's best admirals. It was his mother, married three times in all, who caused the monument to Palmes Fairborne, enriched by an epitaph from the pen of John Dryden, to be installed in the Abbey Nave. She lies nearby, accompanied by her last husband, son to the Earl of Yarmouth.

Piercy Kirke's Finest Hour

Reinforcement of success is the basis of all strategy. The success of the last month's operations was plain to see but more sinews of war were needed before the next phase of any plan to rid Tangier of its perpetual curse could be carried out. Colonel Sackville had, in his field force, a good sword, though the loss of nearly 500 good men, about a quarter of them killed, had reduced its strength. With this in his hand it did mot matter too much that his shield was of poor quality. Beckman, the very professional engineer, had told his friend Colonel George Legge in a letter that 'We have not above six cannons about town, three is broke, no gunners worth bread, no garrison so neglected, materials begins to grow scarce', and Beckman understood these things. The additional companies for the Tangier Regiment were known to be coming, but that was all.

The King was fiercely anxious to back up his soldiers and was not afraid to say so. On 21 October, six days before the last fight, he had opened Parliament and in the course of his speech had vigorously asserted the need to defend the colony. In the last weeks, however, interest in Tangier had been displaced by affairs nearer home. Lord Shaftesbury and the Green Ribbon were in full cry, the Exclusion Bill was introduced on 4 November and before the month was out Lord Stafford was sentenced to death for the crime of adhering to the

old faith. The King could no more save Stafford than he could save
Tangier and up and down the country there was open talk of civil
war. King Charles cut down his household, reduced his garrisons and
sold the royal mews. It made no difference to the garrison; yet again it
would have to do what it could with what it had. Rank and fashion
lost interest and those already in Tangier took passage home as fast as
they could. Colonel Tollemache, whose return was entirely legitimate since he bore an account of the battle written by Mr Shere for
the King, arrived in London two days before Lord Stafford's trial
began. It was not the King's fault that he had no comfort for him, fortunately for Tangier, the Alcaid was now anxious for peace and was
willing to pay heavily rather than have the terrible redcoats launched
at him again. By coincidence a letter from King Charles to Alcaid
Omar, apparently suggested by Lord Inchiquin some time before,
reached the Moorish leader on 19 November and he accepted the
terms offered without any attempt to haggle. Sackville was left to
work out the details, the broad outline being that peace should break
out for six months and Muley Ismail should receive King Charles's
ambassador with all honour. The usual terms about purchasing provisions, grazing cattle in the valleys, fishing and cutting wood without
molestation prevented no difficulty. Sackville wanted none of the old
forts back for, as he wrote to the King, unless he could have 'ten
thousand foot and eight hundred or one thousand horse, it is impossible ever to possess that ground that must be had before these
fortifications can be made according to the draft sent His Majesty'.
The cost would be £300,000 a year for ten years, a sum which
Sackville 'doubts not is too large for His Majesty's undertaking'. It is
doubtful whether the King could have put his hand on as much as a
ha'pence. The treaty, which contained undertakings to give the
Alcaid 100 barrels of powder and as many muskets, also provided that
Captain Fortrey of the Guards should reside at Tetuan as a hostage.
There is no mention of the release of any of the slaves. Nowhere have
I been able to find news of the fate of Captain Trelawny's small son.

A few days before Christmas 1680 the last new companies, to
complete a second battalion for the Tangier regiment, straggled

into the shelter of the Mole. They had had a terrible journey, buffeted by foul winds and mountainous waves to such an extent that several officers and some fifty soldiers had died from accident or sickness on the way. The new regiment soon became known as Trelawny's, when Major Charles Trelawny took it over from the original commander, Colonel Kirke.

Piercy Kirke was the most colourful character to emerge from all the writings on the colony of Tangier. His last post had been as a troop leader in the Blues, from which it is fair to assume that he must have been known to the King[14]. Certainly he was the quintessential Restoration figure, foul-mouthed, lecherous, brave, highly experienced after two campaigns under Turenne and immensely popular with the soldiers in spite of the harsh discipline he maintained.

He was afraid of neither man nor devil but only his wife. Lady Mary Kirke daughter to the Earl of Suffolk, had been a famous beauty and according to camp gossip, she was not so very different from the colonel save that her language was a more refined. The last notable in the party was the ambassador-designate to Fez. Sir James Leslie was a strange choice for, according to Colonel Sackville, he had at one time served as a private trooper in the Tangier horse.

Leslie seems to have allowed his promotion to go to his head. Within a few days of his arrival he was demanding that Colonel Sackville give his reasons in writing for entering into a treaty which Sir James considered disadvantageous. Sackville was prouder of having being able to drive so good a bargain than he was of his recent success in the field and can hardly have taken it kindly to be told that had the new Ambassador been present 'he would never have condescended to that agreement'. He may well have shared the feeling, which he attributed to the Alcaid in a report now with the State Papers, that the Ambassador was 'not so well-born a person as his high mind expected to have come'. The reasons in writing, shorn of their polite phraseology, are unanswerable. With a garrison of no more than 1,500 men on their feet, Tangier was indefensible for any length of time against determined attack. Sir James should reckon himself lucky that the terms were as good as they were. If he were to order the war to be resumed then Colonel Sackville would obey his orders as coming from the King: but he had better think about the shortages of everything before giving such orders. Sir James gave no such orders.

While this was going on, letters arrived for the Alcaid from Muley Ismail. He ratified the treaty and asked that the Ambassador come to him at once. Sir James was not anxious to go until the King's presents for the Emperor should have arrived, but Alcaid Omar had not the hardihood to temporize with his Lord. A compromise was reached: Colonel Kirke should set out at once for Meknes as a kind of herald, making it plain that rich gifts and the Ambassador would be close behind.

Piercy Kirke was in every way fitted for the task. He had a fine presence, he was no enemy to magnificence and there was no Moor in heathendom likely to outface him. He could drink most men under the table and his cultivated mind pretty certainly employed itself in contemplating the novelties in the way of fornication that awaited him. Such talents should not be, nor were they, wasted. Piercy Kirke and Muley Ismail hit it off immediately. The Emperor's taste lay rather for ingenious cruelty and building the palaces and gardens which led one writer to describe Meknes as the Versailles of Morocco. Abundant shaped masonry was at hand in the ruins of Roman Volubilis; equally abundant free labour was available, some of it still recognisable as captured British soldiers. Apart from that, he and Kirke had much in common. Muley Ismail laid on a performance by his cavalry which an old Blues officer watched with commendable solemnity; only his letters show how hard put to it he had been to keep a straight face. So well did the two men get on together that the Emperor was soon saying that Tangier should have peace not for six months but for four years, 'and if he were informed of any breach of the peace by his officers, he would punish them with extreme severity'. Alcaid Omar, who was present for most of the time, was bidden to escort Kirke on to Fez and to show him the city. It is recorded that Omar gave Kirke 'an English boy who was his slave' and who had been useful as interpreter. Unfortunately he is nowhere identified. One can only hope that it was young Trelawny.

There were those who pursed their lips and shook their heads on learning of the private life of the colonel. It was, however, monastic when contrasted with that of his opposite number. Philip Guedalla tells of it feelingly in his description of Mequinez (the spelling is optional) given in 'A Gallery'. Slave labour, great Roman columns, the revenues of Morocco, and Christian prisoners taken under every flag by Sallee pirates were all poured into the work; and Muley Ismail crouched in the shade as the stones swung into place. Sometimes he worked in the long line of chanting slaves or ate his couscous among the brick heaps. That Sultan, with his women and his negro guard and his 700 sons, was a singular intrusion of the fabulous East into the polite age of Louis XIV. The two of them were palace builders. But while fine ladies were admiring the elegant proportions of Versailles, far away to the south Muley Ismail was riding out under his new arches to keep order in Morocco. He kept it with a black army, a strict adherence to the Word, and a personal aptitude for killing which rose to strange heights of homicidal virtuosity. A nervous gentleman from Versailles counted, during a mission of three weeks, forty-seven decapitations by the sovereign to whom he was accredited; and the embarrassed consul at Sallee informed his blushing government that the blood royal of Morocco had received thirty-five additions in forty days. Even Piercy Kirke could not compete with this and, probably inevitably, abandoned the struggle.

The capital and its governor went out of their way to give pleasure to the envoys. Kirke was shown over the palaces and dined with all ceremony; inevitably the only drink served was water but the women of Fez have always been reckoned the best of their kind and Moorish hospitality had its traditions to keep up. Piercy Kirke enjoyed himself hugely. Three days later he was back in Meknes, still in high favour since the Emperor was now insisting that so long as Piercy remained in Tangier 'there should never be any gun fired at the place but that it should be furnished with provisions and the benefits of a hearty peace'. No such language had ever before been heard from an Emperor of Morocco and the price of 'some few guns for his own shooting' was a very small one. Kirke wrote happily to Sackville that the Alcaid 'is the best man in the world and if he had been my own brother he could not have exceeded the kindness he has shown to us all'. Even so he felt it to be time that he got back to Lady Mary. The same letter says that he hopes Sir James Leslie will soon arrive and that if he went about things the right way they could get what they wanted. It was essential to the survival of the colony to play along with the Moors for 'their numbers will always recompense their defect of discipline'. Sackville wrote privately to the commissioners that he wished they would send an Ambassador of better quality than Leslie and he was probably right. Leslie went to Fez early in March 1681, taking his presents from the King, but he did not excite the same warmth of feeling as his harbinger had done. Muley Ismail soon passed him on to the Alcaid; they reached no agreement and when Sir James presented a document proposing that things should remain as they were until the King's pleasure was known it was returned to him cut and torn. In the end, to Leslie's disgust, he had to come away with the ratification of Sackville's terms extended to the period of four years. One cannot help feeling that Piercy Kirke might have done better. The Emperor knew himself to be dealing with a man of little importance and treated him accordingly. He would never have so insulted his friend Piercy. Leslie did try to ransom the prisoners, noted as seventy soldiers and sixty others (probably captured sailors), but the Alcaid would release all or none, at 200 pieces of eight a head. As such a sum could not be found the unfortunates had to be left to their fate.

Early in May both Sackville and Leslie went home, leaving Kirke in command. The Emperor, bored with having no war, claimed that the death of Philip IV of Spain made him legatee of the post of Marmora and he laid siege to it. The garrison soon surrendered on terms and 100 guns changed hands. Muley Ismail looked wistfully at Tangier, observing that if he wanted it he could make himself master of it in a single night; this was only slight exaggeration but it seems that regard for his friend put him in the unusual position of keeping his promise of peace.

Kirke was under no illusions about the value of the treaty. He personally surveyed every inch of the defences and sent home a detailed report on their condition; it makes melancholy reading, though it is not as depressing as Beckman's account. Much work needed doing but there is no suggestion of the place being indefensible.

The state continued that was neither war nor peace. The cattle grazed, the fishermen fished and the grass-cutters brought in forage but on any walk around the ramparts men could see the twinkling of steel on every hill. Pay was now nearly two years in arrears for the old hands, the newcomers had long since run out of money and everybody lived on credit as best he could. It was from about this time that the moral deterioration of Tangier began: drink of a kind could nearly always be got and Colonel Kirke, though fierce in other matters of discipline, did not seem to mind drunkenness, at least so long as a man could remain upright on parade.

At home affairs were becoming worse. By March 1681 the King, having dissolved an impossible Parliament, was existing somehow on subventions from his cousin of France. At the same time King Louis was surreptitiously helping to keep Kara Mustafa in the field and the Turks were making serious plans for the seizure of Vienna. To balance his accounts, the King of France quietly annexed Luxemburg, Strasbourg and Courtrai; in Spain the throne now held its last Hapsburg, the deformed and imbecilic Carlos II. It was not a time propitious for empire-building in Africa and people were becoming bored with Tangier. It paid no dividends, though it made the fortunes of some including Samuel Pepys, now under a cloud. The Mole, it was now being said, would never stand up to Atlantic weather and even if it did it was of no use to anybody. The Royal Navy was in poor shape. Admiral Herbert, still from time to time in Tangier Bay, was not alone in using it for his own purposes, charging heavy rates to merchants for the use of the King's ships as a kind of maritime Securicor. The Duke of York, always a good friend to Tangier, was in trouble enough of his own now that the struggle for the succession was at crisis point and no help could be had from him. The garrison and the townspeople, who still kept up the farce of being a kind of distant Ramsgate with mayor, recorder and the rest, could only live from day to day, adding a little more to the slate at each sundown. The soldiers, bored but still professional, kept up their duties. Guards on the forts were properly changed, patrols and inlying piquets functioned as usual and such as had a mind for it kept up the usual off-duty relaxations of drinking and gambling, quarrelling and whoring.

On one matter, reckoned important by British soldiers of all times, records are silent. It seems almost impossible that 1,500 men, vigorous and healthy, should have had no sports with which to keep themselves amused during long periods of leisure. Possibly no recorder of events thought so trivial a thing worth a mention, for it is hard to believe that the long-established games of an England still rustic were totally neglected. There is nothing to suggest that officers hunted even in the rudest way, that the Guards played football or Dumbarton's Scotch laid out a golf course. It must all be a matter of guesswork, but it is hard to believe that nothing at all was done, even though it was not yet considered any part of an officer's business to organise games, let alone take part in them. Neither have their songs or jokes come down to us; certainly political bawdry like 'Macninny' and 'The Raree Show' survive but these are not the stuff of Sergeant's Mess smokers. All that remains is 'The Grenadiers Rant' in the Roxburghe Ballads, which is a pity.

Colonel Kirke has left behind him an evil reputation, largely as a result of events that then lay years ahead. Nevertheless he was by no means wholly a bad man. The documents dealing with his time as governor show that he made very serious efforts to get the prisoners released, but here he was running his head against a brick wall. Gifts of cloth, attempts to trade captured Moors for captured Christians and promises of future largesse all failed to move Muley Ismail, for on this subject he was immoveable. When a valuable hostage turned up in the shape of his own nephew seeking asylum the Emperor wanted him badly enough to make the Alcaid send his secretary into the city to discuss terms. Alcaid Omar made it very plain that it was futile to talk of an exchange but implored Kirke to return the young man (who in any event had changed his mind and wanted to go back) because he himself would be punished if he failed to get him. Rather than provide *casus belli* Kirke gave in. For the Alcaid the release came too late: on 3 November he died of poison, pretty certainly dispensed by his master. Omar ben Haddo had become too powerful for comfort. His death caused no tears in Tangier for Kirke had already told the garrison, 'that he was the chief, if not the only man, who opposed the interests of this place'. He had certainly been a formidable enemy.

Kirke too was in trouble with his masters. Apparently he had made a bargain under which Moorish prisoners were exchanged for cattle, a deal that would have appealed to his sense of humour as well as having practical advantages, but it earned him a severe reprimand from the Council. In a letter from Whitehall sent on 5 September he was ordered to stop all such transactions until the Emperor should have sent his ambassador, an event long expected but constantly put off. On 21 November news came in from the new Alcaid, brother of the late Omar, that arrival was imminent and Kirke prepared a proper reception. On 23 November 1681, in the middle of the forenoon, the batteries thundered out in salute, the drawbridge at Catherine Port was let down and Colonel Kirke rode out with the escort. It was the best military parade yet seen in Tangier, a worthy start to the centuries of ceremonial that goes naturally with the regular army. Four troops of the Tangier horse led, followed by fifty picked men of Dumbarton's, thirty gunners in new uniforms and '30 negroes in painted coats'. Then came Piercy Kirke, an imposing figure made more so by his own suite of '20 gentlemen well mounted, and 6 men of the tallest stature on each side of his horse, armed with long fusils'. By Fountain Fort the ambassador waited with 200 horsemen armed with lances. On the coming of the governor they gave their traditional salute of a ragged *feu-de-joie* and the leaders exchanged compliments. Only one thing marred the surface cordiality. Piercy Kirke drew the line at receiving a renegade Englishman named Lucas, twice a deserter from the garrison, as an honoured guest in his capacity of Ambassador's secretary. The Alcaid, seeing that in some things Kirke too could be immoveable, agreed to leave him out of the party. He and his retinue made their adieux and the Ambassador's suite was escorted through the walls. More salutes were fired from Peterborough Tower and the puzzled Moor was introduced to another English tradition, a long and boring speech from the mayor. This over, he was led down through the narrow, cobbled streets of the market to the Parade Ground by the Mole, their way being lined by redcoats of the Tangier Regiment's two battalions and Dumbarton's Scotch.

Drawn up on the Parade were two more battalions and the town militia, upon whom Guards instructors had obviously been working. In front of the castle stood the Guards themselves, the four troops of horse that had formed the escort having arrived and formed to their flank. The officers alone saluted as the ambassador passed to the foot of the stairs; there his way was flanked by gunners with glowing linstocks on one side and dismounted troopers with carbines on the other. Kirke led the ambassador through his quarters on to the castle balcony from where they could see the whole town, the bay and the Mole. As the Moor stepped out each regiment in turn fired the traditional three volleys. If this did not convince the delegation that Tangier was the back of a porcupine rather than the paunch of a rabbit nothing would do so. It could not have been better done on the Horse Guards. And nothing even hinted that it was an exercise in papering over cracked walls. The ambassador was captivated and stayed on for a week, rather to Kirke's disgust as he was an expensive and demanding guest. A letter went ahead to Secretary Jenkins warning him that 'no trust or credit should be given to the bare word (though ever solemnly given) of the Morocco Ambassador and his people'. The embassy left in mid-December, arriving at Deal on the last day of the year; Sir James Leslie met them there, writing at once to Jenkins that 'the Moor wished to go to London by land as he has suffered much from the sea voyage'.

The Camden Society copy of the Secret Service accounts reveal that the King had made provision of 1,350 guineas for presents: presumably it came out of King Louis' donative.

Kirke took advantage of this skin-deep bonhomie to return to the subject of the captives. For a time it looked as if he might be getting somewhere but always, when a final bargain seemed near, something happened to cause Muley Ismail to change his tune. It seems probable that he never had the slightest intention of parting with one of them but was amusing himself by teasing his friend Piercy and getting a steady flow of gifts as earnest of the garrison's good intentions. Kirke, almost totally dependent on the hinterland for food and forage, dared not press matters too hard in the face of delicate hints that both could be cut off at a moment's notice. Captain St John, no longer as young as he had once been, petitioned the King and Kirke forwarded the document on. The 'Humble petition of Captain Thomas St John of the old Regiment in Tangier' began by reciting that its writer

> hath been these eight and twenty years (as well in France and Flanders as in Tangier) an officer in Your Majesty's service, which he preferred before a company of Particulars from Don John of Austria, in Flanders, of which Your Majesty was pleased to take notice and both in Bruges and Brussels courteously to assure your Petitioner of a future care of his fortune, of which (in the lowest submission to Your Majesty's pleasure) he now takes the liberty to put your Majesty in mind.

St John reminds his King how:

> at Charles Fort I endured seven weeks siege and suffered a mine to be sprung sooner than yield the Fort, and, when all hopes of relief failed, freely sacrificed my life sooner than deliver the arms and ammunition that were in the Fort to the power of the enemy to oppress the town, in

which attempt I received a musket shot through the body, whereof scarce cured, when through pressing necessity, Sir P. Fairborne would have me officiate as Comptroller of Ordnance, in discharging which by accident of a gun that split I received twenty two wounds, under which I suffered fifteen months together, but much more under the misfortune that I should be the man alone that His Majesty should neglect on such an occasion, whereof I accuse more my own unlucky planet than the King's bounty, having none to put him in mind of it.

All the unlucky St John asked for was promotion to a vacant majority; whether the King did anything for an old companion of his travels seems doubtful. St John's signature appears in a petition dated October 1683; he was still 'T. St. John, Capt'.

As the cry of 'nest of Papists' was becoming even more strident at home it is worth mentioning that Kirke at about this time sent Captain McKenny on leave, 'to put himself right with the King, who had been told that he was a Roman Catholic, and he is desirous of disproving it and taking the oath of allegiance and supremacy', Kirke had a good opinion of him, and said so. If any nest existed it seems to have escaped the notice of people highly placed in Tangier.

No writer has any good to say of Piercy Kirke and plainly he was not a man whom everyone would invite to tea. For all that, there was not much wrong with his professional skill and diligence. His detailed standing orders are still with the Dartmouth MSS and it is hard to improve upon them. The custom, still with us, of standing-to before dawn and dusk had already acquired a respectable antiquity by the 1680s but it was Kirke who added much to such ordinary precautions. Great responsibilities were put upon the sentry on Peterborough Tower. If he saw a party of ten or more of the enemy on foot, he must hoist a blue flag; for similar parties of horse a red one; if 'he perceive them to increase numerous', up was to go 'the great flagge, not taking in the other two'. For ships he was to send up one, two or three balls, depending on their numbers, and the 'great flagge' signalled that they were making for the city. The alarm was to be given by the great bell in the tower, taken up by the drums and every unit, sub-unit and man knew exactly where to go and what to do. Every day each battalion had to exercise all its men not on guard, details of Grand and Visiting Rounds were set out plainly and, for the horse, there were two-hourly patrols around the boundaries. In case of surprise it was open to anyone to fire three rounds in succession, on hearing which all hands were to act as if the bell had tolled. There were distinctive signals for summoning individual units, ten bell-strokes for the Guards, twenty for Dumbarton's, thirty for the Tangier regiment (confusingly, and frequently, called the Governor's), forty for Trelawny's and a special small bell for gunners alone. These were not merely written orders of the kind sometimes produced by commanders wishing only to cover themselves in case of accident. Kirke rigorously kept his officers and men at practice until the business became second nature; then they practised again. To such a commander much is forgiven. His relationship with Muley Ismail was useful for nipping small incidents in the bud; whenever the Alcaid tried to 'work a flanker' by threatening to cut off supplies were he not given guns, powder, cloth or whatever he fancied for the moment, Kirke had only to say that he would at once complain to the Emperor at such lack of Arab honour and there it ended. He was also a fair man to his subordinates. Ensign Elliott was cashiered after some quarrel.

He promptly enlisted in the ranks, served as a private soldier in his old company and made a good ranker. After a decent interval, when he had purged his contempt, he was sent home, taking with him a letter from Kirke to the King recommending that he be given the next ensign's commission to fall vacant.

Tangier, however, had only a short time left to it. The ambassador returned from England in August 1682, bringing with him what was called the Whitehall Treaty. It confirmed all Kirke's suspicions. All the Moorish prisoners, the bulk of his labour for repairing the Mole and the fortifications, were to be handed back without any Christians being given in exchange. Kirke was expected, said the ambassador, to back the bill he had given for a quantity of powder which he had brought but not paid for. Kirke refused to do anything of the kind: when an attempt was made by the Alcaid and the renegade Lucas to overpower the crew and sail the powder-ship away, Kirke turned the Mole batteries on it. The ambassador arrived at Fez empty-handed, was 'most cruelly treated' and the Emperor demanded that the Duke of Albemarle, of whose existence he had that moment learned, be sent to him as envoy for King Charles.

This was the most deadly moment of the entire Tangier story and it displayed the young regular army at its best. Pay was fourteen months overdue, the magazines were nearly empty and there were so few men that Kirke was forced to use his soldiers to carry out essential labourers' work. The sort of conditions, in fact, that future generations would come to expect. It was like living with an unexploded mine under the parade ground; at any minute it might go off but until that happened there was nothing for it but to carry on with the ordinary duties of the day. Colonel Kirke performed his share of them to the full but, like a sensible officer, he was at pains to keep himself fit. A good cellar helped, as did a little bathing-house with its resident houri. When Lady Mary's sister came to spend a visit her host ensured that she went home in an interesting condition. Though not in the league of Muley Ismail, Piercy Kirke was never an idle man.

The Mole had already cost well over £1,000,000; something in the order of £70,000 a year was leaving London and, as it did not find its way into the soldiers' pockets, it was plainly being converted to other uses. In December the garrison numbered 3,411 officers and men, the Guards making up 379 of them, Dumbarton's two battalions another 916, the two Tangier battalions contributing nearly 1,400 and the rest being made up of 'Capt. Bassett's Miners' and thirty-three gunners. The view now held in England was that the keeping of such a garrison for no purpose other than protecting a few hundred civilians of no outstanding serviceability to the country hardly made much sense. In addition to everything else there was no help to be expected from Christendom. Muley Ismail was something more than an Oriental barbarian; he was, says Philip Guedalla, in correspondence with Louis XIV, of a nature friendly enough to warrant his request for a French princess to be added to his collection. Later on the elderly Emperor was to offer James the use of a black army paid by Morocco should he care to invade England and there set up the true faith. Islamic fundamentalism is not a recent growth. The fact of the matter was that Tangier had become no longer capable of defending itself against an enemy grown formidable.

So large a population in so small a place demands a lot of water; cut it off, and the town could not hold out for a day. The carefully planned ways of ekeing out supplies matured over the centuries by the Portuguese, kept deadly secret and committed to writing only the once, had vanished when Lord Peterborough mislaid the book long ago. Now, if Fountain Fort were to be lost, the drinking water supply would be lost with it. It might well be that one red-coat was worth a regiment of Moors, but it would only be so for as long as he had a full canteen. Tangier was now held on sufferance, sustained only by the Emperor's promise of a four-year peace, a promise that might be disavowed at any minute. The probable consequences were the stuff of nightmares.

By the summer of 1683 even the King was convinced of the ineluctable necessity of giving the place up. He loathed the idea of abandoning it but was realistic enough to know that he lacked the means to keep it and his troubles were now so serious that the presence of veteran regiments under his own hand would be welcome. Though he took few people into his confidence, King Charles began to prepare a plan for evacuation with as little ignominy as possible. It was to resemble Gallipoli more than Aden. The city and its inhabitants were not to be handed over as a going concern to whichever local potentate made the most noise; every living soul would be removed, the works destroyed and, if Muley Ismail cared to take over, he would not get much joy of it.

The governor was not made privy to what was in the air. He still corresponded wearily with Muley Ismail who was becoming more captious every day. He refused to do business with anybody other than Piercy Kirke for whom he plainly still retained a liking. Even when their messages to each other were most acid, mostly on the subject of the captives, he allowed himself to say that he wished Kirke were of his religion, 'for thy discretion, courtesy and wisdom has given thee an entry into my heart, and I never desired any Christian to be of my religion but thyself'. Kirke replied ambiguously that should he ever think of making a change, he would become a Muslim. Despite all efforts, in-fighting became more frequent as tempers gave way under strain and duels were fought more often than ever before. Happily all this coincided with an event that took off some of the pressure. Muley Ismail went to war with his nephew Muley Achmet and had advanced so far into the interior towards Sus that he became stuck, unable to go forward or back.

In July 1683 the King, having finally made up his mind, handed his written commission to George Legge, Earl of Dartmouth. He was to have practically the entire fleet put at his disposal, was to sail with it to Tangier, assume the office of governor, destroy the Mole and the fortifications, and bring away every man, woman and child. Compensation for losses was to be assessed and paid. For this part of the work Lord Dartmouth pressed into service a man who needed only to see Tangier to know all about it. Samuel Pepys came aboard HMS *Grafton* at Portsmouth.

11
Lord Dartmouth

On 14 July 1683 the army of Kara Mustafa arrived before the glacis of Vienna and began work on the most elaborate system of trenches ever yet seen. Levies had been got together from every Ottoman bashalik and with work of this kind to be done it seems probable that the Turkish-Cretan miners who had ruined the prospects for Tangier were present under the horse-tail banner. This was just as well for that city's chances of a decorous evacuation. At the same time Lord Dartmouth was equally busy at Portsmouth, fitting out every vessel that was capable of transporting men and gear.

Late in August twenty-one ships, led by the navy's pride, HMS *Grafton*, passed the Lizard outward bound. Nine were men-of-war, the rest empty transports. Ten more merchantmen kept rendezvous there. The outward voyage took just over three weeks, about par for the course, and on 14 September the leaders made fast alongside the Great Mole. From the deck of the flagship Mr Pepys took stock of the place that had done so much for him, his friends and relations. His former clerk Will Hewer was Treasurer – his signature appears frequently in the State Papers – his seldom-do-well brother-in-law Balty St Michel enjoyed the perquisites of being navy agent and but for Tangier Pepys would have been a poor man. Like everybody else he was enraptured by the distant prospect and the spicy smells wafted from the land but before his foot had touched the Mole Mr Pepys was aghast at what he saw. 'But Lord, how could ever anybody think this place fit to be kept in this charge, that by its being overlooked by so many hills can never be secured against an enemy', he confided to his diary. It was a little late in the day for such animadversion.

The men charged with the destruction of Tangier had all been sent home earlier in order to settle details with the King and were now returning. Mr Shere and Major Beckman were with Pepys and Lord Dartmouth on board *Grafton* and had worked out the details. To Beckman, honest mercenary that he was, it was simply another job; for Henry Shere it must have come near to heart-break, planning how best to destroy the most stupendous pieces of engineering seen since the Romans. In public, at any rate, he displayed admirable fortitude. As much care and skill went into arrangements for the devastation as had gone into construction. Piercy Kirke, too, made no fuss about what had to be done when all was made plain to him at a dinner given on board by his supplanter. Possibly the presence at table of the chaplain, the future Bishop Kerr of pious memory, prevented him from saying what naturally rose to his lips. Pepys says that he gave excellent advice; he could hardly have failed to know the governor's reputation but at this point he seems quite to have warmed to him.

To a soldier it is axiomatic that, in withdrawal, running fights must be avoided. Each formed body must retire through another, leap-frogging all the way until only the last may have to abandon dignity and run for it. There seemed no certainty that this would be possible as the Moors knew what was going on – at the sight of so many ships they could hardly have done otherwise – and were daily becoming bolder and more insolent. Their sentries were now shouting pleasantries about blowing the place up and, more sinister, they seemed for the first time to be tampering with the water supply. The Spaniards were expressing heavy displeasure at the spectacle of this great fleet and were giving 'great provocations'. At sea the Barbary Corsairs had been unusually active lately and a number of English merchantmen had been snapped up. Kirke had had a meeting with the Alcaid on neutral ground a month before the fleet arrived at which the Moor had been evasive, grumbling about the absence of gifts which he claimed to have been promised and making every possible difficulty over selling cattle, permitting grazing and quarrying and all the other things that had caused so much friction over the years. Without his sappers the Alcaid could not mount a serious attack but he could make himself a very considerable nuisance, for Dartmouth was going to need every mouthful of food he could get locally for the voyage home. The Alcaid had to be kept sweet for a few weeks and only Piercy Kirke could look after this. He succeeded pretty well, partly with a broad hint that should the Alcaid start anything at Tangier Admiral Herbert's ships would blow the port of Sallee off the map. This gave the Moor food for thought.

Mr Pepys had the job of evaluating compensation claims, which he began by calling on all landowners to deduce their titles. Conveyancing in Tangier had not been meticulous and the imprecision of much of the evidence tendered aggravated him. He took a hate to Tangier and everybody in it, except for Lady Mary Kirke and his old friend Shere. Soon he could say nothing good about either Kirke or Herbert and he began to compile a *chronique scandaleuse* crammed with scatological detail about their doings. It was probably no more than jealousy. Pepys was a lickerish little man and only want of nerve kept him from becoming their boon companion. Whether they would have welcomed him is another matter. Herbert and Kirke were both professionals, drawing a rigid line between 'on parade' and 'off parade'; Pepys, the quintessential civilian, never understood this.

There were still half a hundred of the enduring molemen left and they were at once put to work by their old master. If any proof were needed of the excellence of what they had done it presented itself now. Great charges of powder were put in place, tamped down and touched off. Clouds of smoke and rubble covered the sun, but the Mole remained. With mixed feelings they tried again. To cover it all Colonel Kirke laid on a show of force. Amongst the gear brought in the ships were new scarlet uniforms for Dumbarton's and Trelawny's, none of which had been issued. For the moment they were lent to the Royal Navy and served to clothe four battalions of 200 men each for the day; fortunately Dumbarton's were not kilted. On 28

September more than 4,000 men marched across the drawbridge at Catherine Port for the last time. The Guards took up station with their right on Pole Fort, Trelawny's, the Tangier Regiment and Dumbarton's prolonging the line eastward in front of Cambridge and Fountain with the Naval Brigade drawn up on the beach. Behind Trelawny's a battery of guns took action stations, guard boats covered the sea, the frigates ran out their guns and the militia lined the walls. At the sight of this powerful array the Alcaid rode down with his usual rout to enquire what it all meant. While courtesies were being exchanged a stage army of oddments marched to and fro, giving the impression that the force was even greater than it seemed. The demonstration served its end as the new governor explained to the Secretary, 'I thought this appearance more to the purpose than entering into cavilings with them, and it succeeded as I desired, for they have lived extremely well with us ever since'.

Although the decision to evacuate was irrevocable, Lord Dartmouth appointed a commission under Mr Shere to make a last examination and report. Their findings were lengthy, detailed and possibly coloured by a desire to justify what was being done. Essential works would cost £1,297,201 16s 6d: the cost of an army for twelve years would add another £3,501,561. The army would have to number not less than 2,000 horse and 8,000 foot. Captain Sir John Berry RN examined the Mole and damned it out of hand. The whole place was 'altogether unuseful to His Majesty for receiving, careening or preserving HM ships'. The report bears twenty-seven signatures, one the future Admiral Sir George Rooke, but that of Mr Shere is lacking. The Mole defied all attempts to bring it down, even when Captain Leake, the master gunner of England, personally touched off two bombs under it.

It was on 4 October that the formal proclamation was read in the Market Place. Though, as it said,

> the King has gone to great expense and trouble to make
> it a secure habitation, a commodious harbour, and a place
> for trade to flourish in, yet the results have been so dis-

couraging, and so many brave men's lives have been lost
in the defence of the town, which is now in so ruinous a
state as to make it dangerous to live in owing to the hostility of the Moors.

All the inhabitants would be removed, with their families and goods,
to where they wished to go. The King had given strict orders that the
Portuguese were to be taken off first. It seems that Whitehall at least
half expected the running fight to take place. None of the civil population seemed other than pleased and grateful save for the
Portuguese who were understandably bitter. The only complaint, a
fair one, came from the officers of the Tangier horse. They had had to
buy their mounts in Spain at prices between £30 and £80 apiece;
they were now ordered to return them to that country for sale, flood
the market and lose heavily. Could they not take their chargers home
with them? As none of the loading lists mention horses it seems that
the request must have been refused. The garrison delivered a petition
over the signature of Colonel Kirke and fifty-nine officers saying, in
effect, that they would be glad to see the back of Tangier and could
be of more use to His Majesty at home 'amidst the present just
apprehensions occasioned by the late horrid conspiracy [the Rye
House plot] which still threatens your Royal person and the distur-
bance of your Government'. It ends, 'We shall never unworthily use
those swords Your Majesty has been pleased to put into our hands,
but employ them for the preservation and honour of Your Majesty's
Sacred Person and your Royal service to the last drop of our blood'.
Sir James Leslie seems to have returned to his old service, for one of
the signatures is his, now as a simple major of horse. Apparently he
went home to Scotland immediately afterwards.

In accordance with the King's promise the Portuguese, about
sixty all told, were taken off first, as their descendants were to be
taken from other African possessions nearly three centuries later.
Then, on 15 October, came something of a shock. The Emperor,
having extricated himself from his family quarrel, wrote to Lord
Dartmouth. English ships had been sinking and capturing Moorish

ships – which was true – and he was therefore mustering an army and intended war. Lord Dartmouth was undismayed and so replied. If Muley Ismail wanted one last fight he could not have chosen a better moment. 253 useless mouths left the same day under 'John Eccles, usher and gunner', consigned to Pendennis Castle. On 5 November, anniversary of past Gunpowder Plot and future landing of William at Torbay, the last ship, the *Swan*, left with thirty passengers for Marseilles. In all, eight transports were at sea carrying 262 men, and 349 women and children. On the last day of October the Mole finally succumbed, the explosion setting fire to a house in which Mr Hewer lived. It belonged to Captain St John, unlucky to the last. The combined efforts of 2,000 men, had been needed for the work of destruction, and it was still far from complete.

The closing days of Tangier were amongst the unhappiest. Discipline began to relax, probably helped by the ease in getting at wine and spirits left behind. Kirke, praying friendship in aid for the last time, tried hard to persuade Muley Ismail to let his captives go. As usual, he got no straight answer. Mr Shere had said, with a mixture of pride and desperation all that remained was to keep strict guard and under its cover to complete the systematic wrecking of everything.

Winter set in early that year, adding wind and rain to the short commons and heavy work which were now the garrison's portion. Men huddled into greatcoats before venturing out into the deserted streets and slipped cursing as they struggled up and down the steep little hills to their work at undermining the fortifications they had held so faithfully and so long. Everybody had gone, from the mayor and recorder pompous in their scarlet and ermine to Joyce the pretty little whore who was said to have infected no less than 400 of them. Colonel Kirke, says Pepys, had been much entertained by finding that his own secretary 'was one that got it most pockly'. The rain, however, was not wholly a curse, for the summer had been a dry one and the downpour put an end to worries about the water supply. It also reduced the risk of surprise attacks for the Moors never fancied fighting in the wet.

Kirke was a stronger character than Dartmouth and local affairs were still left largely to him. In the sensible belief that diplomacy was an extension of war by other means he kept up an uninterrupted communication with the Alcaid who was plainly not disposed to carry out the jehad decreed by his Imperial master. Although by nature he was harsh and impatient Kirke kept up a courteous intercourse under great provocation, for the Alcaid could hardly admit that he was letting the Nazrani have things all his own way. Promises for the release of slaves were made and broken with a monotony that must have been infuriating but Kirke kept his temper. Whatever may be urged against him, and there is no shortage of material, Piercy Kirke had good qualities. In money matters he seems to have been tolerably honest for an account over the signature of Will Hewer shows his own pay at November 1682 to have been in arrears to the tune of nearly £4,000. Dr Lawrence, the staff physician, gave it to Pepys as his opinion that 'as to public buildings for the benefit of the place he [Kirke] hath done more than all of [the previous governors] put together'.

Lady Mary, her two daughters and servants stayed until all other non-combatants had gone, only leaving in HMS *Diamond* on 26 November. Ten days later Mr Pepys, his work done, sailed for Spain. It is on the strength of his writings that Tangier has such a bad name; they do not deserve to be treated as Holy Writ. Pepys had never trailed a pike nor experienced the hardship, weariness, pain and fear that pride of regiment overcomes. Living in sheltered England he had never even seen a garrison town, nor did soldiers often come his way except when they were taking their ease. He cannot be blamed for not realizing that under his eyes was the nucleus of the armies with which, only a year after his death, a former ensign of the Tangier Regiment would storm the Schellenberg and begin the long roll of battle honours of the future.

On 20 January 1684 the field officers of the garrison reported to Dartmouth that all the mines were ready. The next day the naval men declared the Mole to be in ruins and the harbour choked with rubble; it could no longer shelter 'pirate, robber or any enemy of the

Christian faith, or any other'. Dartmouth gave the order to fire the charges, after parading the entire garrison just in case the Alcaid or his men might be exalted by religious fervour and come screaming in. There followed a series of earth-shaking explosions, far exceeding anything ever heard before. When the dust settled Pole Fort had ceased to exist and the walls of the town lay as flat as Jericho. Only at Peterborough Tower did some charges fail to ignite and it remained a silent memorial to a generation of wasted effort. As such it did not long endure. Dartmouth warned the Alcaid of the unexploded mine but the Moors took no notice and on entering the city they blew it up, by accident killing eight of their number.

Now the number of the guns was thinned out from the temporary earthworks that housed them; the cavalry was shipped to Cadiz where the horses were to be sold in exchange for rations. Their parade state for 1 February, the day of embarkation, shows a strength of 183 all ranks. Between 8 and 26 February each regiment in turn marched by companies – of about platoon size – to the beach and were ferried to the seventeen ships waiting for them in the roadstead. No particular order of precedence seems to have been followed and there was some trans-shipping in the Bay of Bulls off Cadiz. Nobody was sorry to see the wreckage of Tangier sink out of sight, least of all the five prisoners whom Kirke had managed to have freed from Tetuan.

When he saw the last topsails dip below the horizon the Alcaid, for what motive one cannot tell, decided to free all the survivors. Thirty-eight men from around Tangier and eleven more from Sallee were handed over to Captain Langston, whose ship presumably had been left behind for a last clearing-up. Heading the list is that Lieutenant Wilson, whose captivity had lasted three years and ten months since Henrietta Fort went under. The survival record was held by Thomas Nicholls, soldier, taken from a Tangier boat. He had endured for twelve years and seven months. John Clover, seaman taken from 'Good Hope, a small ship of London', had notched up exactly ten years. The English colony of Tangier had ceased to exist.

Epilogue

The Tangier garrison was soon absorbed into the army list. The Guards returned to Whitehall, the Tangier horse became the 1st Royal Dragoons; the old Tangier or Governor's Regiment was reborn as the 2nd Foot, the Queen's Royal West Surreys: Dumbarton's, already a British regiment became the 1st, The Royal Scots, and Trelawny's the 4th, The King's Own (Lancaster). The Queen's most undeservedly were soon to come by the unflattering name of Kirke's Lambs after the Bloody Assize. It was a business with which Kirke certainly had something to do but the 2nd Foot had no part in it. Nor, with all respect to Lord Macaulay, did they assume the badge of lamb and flag until some time after the landing of King William.

Was the whole adventure worth while? It is impossible to be certain. Bombay proved the key to an Empire in India but the two places are totally dissimilar. Had King Charles been given not Bombay but Karachi it might have gone the same way as Tangier. Probably the fate of Tangier was settled far away. Had there been peace in Europe, had the Treasury been full, it is not unimaginable that a large force might have pushed the boundaries far out, persuaded the inhabitants of the benefits of civilization and established a thriving new land. More probably, however, the total antipathy of Crescent for Cross would have made it impossible. The attempt has to be written down to experience; the difference between Tangier and other African possessions taken by Europeans from weaker inhabitants is that it lasted for decades rather than centuries. Its benefits were purely military. The professional skill and discipline of the repatriated Tangier garrison leavened the very amateur forces at home; without them Monmouth might have prevailed at

Sedgmoor and it is hard to see how the armies of Queen Anne could have reached the near-perfection that enabled them to settle the fate of Europe. The millions of pounds cast on the waters by King Charles were found after many days.

The city and its hinterland slowly reverted to the way of life that it had enjoyed for centuries past. Petty monarch fought it out with petty monarch, the outside world drew in its skirts until barbarism went a little too far in its treatment of Christians and punishment was demanded. In 1844 King Louis Philippe, who was marking out the beginnings of a French Empire in North Africa, sent a squadron under the Prince de Joinville to bombard Tangier itself. Nine years later the sloop HMS *Scout*, performing one of those endless duties by which the Royal Navy kept the waters of the world properly charted, paid a visit of a more harmless kind. Her Captain's 'Remarks' are preserved.

After telling of 'the rock on which HMS *Excellent* struck' he told of Tangier Bay also having 'a reef running off some considerable distance which at low water is nearly dry. This reef is the remains of a mole which in the reign of Charles II was blown up previous to evacuating the place. It still, however, answers the purpose and affords good shelter for feluccas and small boats'. All else that remained were 'a few dilapidated forts facing the sea'. Much the same was said forty years later by Stephen Bonsal of the American Central News who accompanied a rather futile trade mission under Sir Charles Euan Smith. Bonsal, anxious to get home quickly in order to write his book, took passage in a felucca and came near to being wrecked on 'the remains of the magnificent Mole the English destroyed on leaving Tangier'. Apart from an occasional mention of this memorial to the men of Whitby, Tangier and everything to do with it faded from memory.

Suddenly, almost exactly two centuries after the evacuation, a British military presence was once more seen on the ramparts of Tangier. It came about in this way. In 1876 the then Sultan of Morocco, Muley Hassan, came to the conclusion that he needed a proper army of 10,000 men, armed, trained and disciplined as never before. For a start he despatched 100 of his best troops to Gibraltar with a request that the garrison there would teach its neighbour how to soldier. Relations between the two powers were less than cordial but when the Sultan asked that a British officer be lent to him for the overseeing of the business he was not given a flat refusal. There were, however, difficulties. Both France and Spain would be mightily offended if a gentleman holding the commission of Queen Victoria were to be seen training or, worse, commanding a Muslim army on Christendom's doorstep. The hour, in accordance with its custom, produced the man. Harry Maclean, son of a Scottish doctor, had just retired after eight years in the infantry and, being without other employment, was very willing to take it on. In 1877 he moved over to Tangier, took up his quarters and, assisted by the original 100, addressed himself to the task. His arrival caused an international stir for it was something quite without precedent. A Scot, a Presbyterian at that, with no command of any tongue but his own was training and was probably going to command a Muslim army, possibly highly militant upon its own soil but within striking distance of the European forces now garrisoning various parts of the littoral. By one means and another Maclean managed his heavy task.

He learned enough Arabic for practical purposes though his Scottish pronunciation was capable of moving a rather solemn people to open laughter, nobody gave him much help. The Sultan's ministers, furiously resentful as might have been expected, did everything they could to render his mission impossible. After a while the Sultan himself began to have doubts. It was all very well to own an efficient army when his gaze was turned outwards at France and Spain and their African possessions. When affairs nearer home came under consideration, however, it looked a little different. Some faithless, unbelieving general might win over the army for himself and, with or without some other aspirant to the throne, march on the palace. He might even declare himself the first Scottish Emperor of Morocco. Better to make sure that the army did not become over-efficient, nor too well equipped with the latest weapons. No objection was raised to the Kaid – Maclean's new title – exercising his main leisure activity of playing the bagpipes on Tangier's ramparts where Piercy Kirke had once walked but that was martial display enough. The Sultan need not have discomposed himself for Harry Maclean was that thing almost unknown to the Maghreb, a man of complete uprightness who could be neither bought nor frightened. The Sultan's form of monarchy was not quite that of Queen Victoria but Maclean had, in the words of Wellington, eaten his salt and was his man. He was also very useful as a kind of connecting-file with the diplomats of Europe, though never once did he come anywhere near to betraying his trust.

At the request of his new sovereign Maclean came to the coronation of King Edward VII as part of the Moroccan delegation. His services were marked by the reward of a knighthood and Sir Harry returned to Tangier where, after a decent interval, he handed over his command to a Moorish officer. After various adventures, including a kidnapping brought about by the schisms that followed his retirement, he settled down in the place that he knew best and loved most. In 1920, within the confines of Queen Catherine's dowry, Harry Maclean, KCMG, died honoured by all and the last link with the British army came to an end.

For all that, the evidence remains. Look at any laid-up Standard of The Royal Dragoons or Colour of The Queen's Regiment and you will remark their first Battle Honour 'TANGIER 1662-1680'. The later arrivals, Grenadiers, Coldstreamers and Royal Scots carry it as 'TANGIER 1680'. The dates are puzzling, as is the omission of The King's Own, but the Battle Honours Committee that so ordered things is long gone and the questions are beyond answering. But, undeniably, this is the first Battle Honour of the British regular army. And no unworthy one.

Notes

1. Fortescue says that this name is something of a mystery. 'Terclo', of course, means a third. But a third of what? Nobody could tell him.
2. Which, in the fullness of time, was to furnish the army with the Dublin Fusiliers and, from Bengal, the Munsters.
3. The French ordered things better. In 1682 a fleet under Duquesne, learning that a French warship had been captured and her commander, the Chevalier de Beaujeu, sold in the slave market, flattened the place. Or very nearly.
4. *Morocco As It Is*, by Stephen Bonsal, Special Correspondent of the Central News 1893.
5. History has not been generous to Catherine of Braganza. King Charles named the borough of Queens in New Amsterdam after her shortly before changing the name of the city to New York. In 1988 a charitable organization known as the Friends of Queen Catherine raised some $2.4 million for the building of a statue of her. Perhaps they should have expected to be told that 'Catherine's hands are bloody with the murder of millions of Africans' and asked 'Do we really need a statue of a slave mistress?', as the Chairman of the Committee against Queen Catherine began her well-expressed views on the proposal. Others were less friendly. *Daily Telegraph* 16 January 1998.
6. The word admiral is, of course, a legacy from the Iberian Emirs: 'Amir al Bahr', Lord of the Sea.
7. The town was sold back to King Louis in October 1662 at the price of five million livres. It was a good bargain for the place, despite its limited usefulness, had been costing over £130,000 a year. The House of Commons, for neither the first nor the last time, affected great indignation at something for which they were privately grateful.
8. Though the next couple of centuries took them to all the places that ever saw a red-coat, the Queen's never forgot their origin. In 1881, when the infantry of the line adopted its county titles, the commanding officer asked permission of the Portuguese ambassador for the use of a Portuguese air as the new regimental march. Two were suggested; they were arranged in 1883 and the fine tune 'Braganza' was formally adopted in 1903. It is seldom heard now, for the Queen's are no more; merely one unit in the Princess of Wales's Royal Regiment.
9. However odd it may seem, Gayland was justified in law. Treaties, unlike private contracts, continue to be binding so as long as the conditions prevailing at the time of their conclusion continue and no longer. The view, shared by Bismarck in 'Gedanken und Erinnungen' ii, p.258 and hallowed by the name of 'Rebus sic stantibus', has long existed and, time and again, states have announced themselves no longer bound when, in their view, things have changed. The doctrine now seems out of fashion.
10. Of all infantry weapons the one least changed over several centuries must be the hand grenade. There is a report in the *Daily Telegraph* for 28 March 1992 of the finding of a Civil War specimen apparently used during the siege of Leicester

Castle in 1645. It was about ten inches in diameter, made of ceramic and with a hole pierced thorough the top for a fuse. Probably as good as the 1941 plastic affair called the No. 69.

11. 'Drop' was, and remains, a well-understood word amongst military engineers for a small detached fort. There still stands a Drop Redoubt amongst the works on the Western Heights at Dover.

12. Some explanation of an extraordinary breach not only of discipline but of good manners appears in Samuel Pepys' diary entry for 24 September 1662. Lord Crewe, he wrote, had advised the committee to 'keep my Lord Sandwich from proceeding too far in the business of Tangier'. The reason given, sensibly enough was that 'the king would not be able to afford building the Mole unless the garrison were reduced'. Then, Lord Crewe argued, the King would have to decide on something rather serious. 'Either Lord Sandwich must oppose the Duke of York, who will have the Irish regiment under Fitzgerald continued or else my Lord Peterborough who is concerned to have the English continued'. The Irish presence was plainly increasing even at this early date and it looked 'as if your Irish officer may have become too big for his boots'.

13. Even as far back as the age of Charles II the army was over-stretched. The 1st, 2nd, and 4th Regiments of Foot served in Tangier. The 3rd (later the Buffs) would have done so but just as it was about to embark news came in of Nathaniel Bacon's rebellion against the detested governor of Virginia, Sir William Berkeley. The rebellion was over by the time they arrived but Sir William was making his presence felt in a way that Tangier would never have tolerated. The King spoke bitterly of it. 'The old fool has killed more people in that naked country than I have done for the murder of my father'. The 3rd Foot never saw Tangier.

Bibliography and Sources

OFFICIAL DOCUMENTS

The Tangier State Papers, Public Record Office, C.O. 279
The Audit Office Declared Accounts for the years in question.
Ordnance Minutes vol. II et seq.
Audit Office Enrolments vol. X

PRINTED BOOKS

West Barbary, or a Short Narrative of the Revolutions of the Kingdom of Fez and Morocco, The Revd Lancelot Addison, Oxford 1671.
A Discourse Touching Tangier: in a letter to a Person of Quality, London 1680.
Money Paid and Received for the Secret Services of Charles II and James II, Camden Society. London 1851.
Cannon's Histories of the lst, The Royal Dragoons, the 2nd and 4th Foot, London 1838–1840.
John Evelyn's Diary
The Life, Journals and Correspondence of Samuel Pepys, John Smith, London 1841.
History of the 2nd Queens, now the Royal West Surrey Regiment Davis, Richard Bentley, 1887.
The Old Seaport of Whitby, Robert Tate Gaskin, 1909.
Morocco As It Is, Stephen Bonsal, W.H. Allen, 1893.
King Charles II, Arthur Bryant, Longmans, 1931.
History of the Standing Army, Clifford, Walton 1897.
Tangier, England's Lost Atlantic Outpost, E.M.G. Routh, 1912.

PAMPHLETS (IN THE BRITISH LIBRARY)

A Brief Relation of the Present State of Tangier etc London 1666.
The Present Danger of Tangier, or an Account of its being Attempted by a Great Army of the Moors by Land etc, In a letter from Cadiz dated 29 July 1679.
A Discourse Touching Tangier, in a Letter to a Person of Quality, London, 1680.
A Particular Relation of the late success of His Majesty's Forces at Tangier, Tangier, 23 September 1680.
Tangier Rescue, or a Relation of the late Memorable Passages at Tangier etc, John Ross, gentleman, London, 1681.

List of Illustrations

1. View of Tangier from the east. From the engraving by Hollar in the Royal Library at Windsor.
2. A view of Tangier looking towards the sandhills. From the original painting by Stoop, in the possession of Lord Dartmouth.
3. The little Mole, showing the wharf and Custom House, 1675. From the original drawing in the Royal Library at Windsor.
4. Tangier Bay, showing the position of the Mole, 1668. From the original drawing in the Royal Library at Windsor.
5. Plan of the Mole at Tangier in 1675. From the original drawing in the Royal Library at Windsor.
6. The Great Chest constructed for the Mole by Mr Shere, 1677. From the original drawing in the Royal Library at Windsor.
7. The ground and forts round Tangier.

Index

REGIMENTS

Battles & Campaigns

A series of illustrated battlefield accounts covering the classical period through to the end of the twentieth century, drawing on the latest research and integrating the experience of combat with intelligence, logistics and strategy.

Series Editor

Hew Strachan, Chichele Professor of the History of War at the University of Oxford

Published

Ross Anderson, *The Battle of Tanga 1914*
William Buckingham, *Arnhem 1944*
Martin Kitchen, *The German Offensives of 1918*
A.J. Smithers, *The Tangier Campaign*
Tim Travers, *Gallipoli 1915*

Forthcoming

Ross Anderson, *The East African Front 1914–18*
Stephen Conway, *The Battle of Bunker Hill 1775*
Brian Farrell, *The Defence & Fall of Singapore 1941–42*
David M. Glantz, *Before Stalingrad: Barbarossa*
Michael K. Jones, *Bosworth 1485*
Martin Kitchen, *El Alamein 1942–43*
M.K. Lawson, *The Battle of Hastings 1066*
Marc Milner, *The Battle of the Atlantic 1939–1945*
John Andreas Olsen, *Operation Desert Storm*
Michael Penman, *Bannockburn 1314*
Matthew C. Ward, *Quebec 1759*